T0316669

Cambridge Elements ≡

Elements in Religion and Violence

edited by

James R. Lewis
Wuhan University

Margo Kitts
Hawai'i Pacific University

CHRISTIANITY AND VIOLENCE

Lloyd Steffen

Lehigh University

CAMBRIDGE
UNIVERSITY PRESS

CAMBRIDGE
UNIVERSITY PRESS

University Printing House, Cambridge CB2 8BS, United Kingdom

One Liberty Plaza, 20th Floor, New York, NY 10006, USA

477 Williamstown Road, Port Melbourne, VIC 3207, Australia

314–321, 3rd Floor, Plot 3, Splendor Forum, Jasola District Centre, New Delhi – 110025, India

79 Anson Road, #06–04/06, Singapore 079906

Cambridge University Press is part of the University of Cambridge.

It furthers the University's mission by disseminating knowledge in the pursuit of education, learning, and research at the highest international levels of excellence.

www.cambridge.org
Information on this title: www.cambridge.org/9781108796699
DOI: 10.1017/9781108859271

First published 2021

A catalogue record for this publication is available from the British Library.

ISBN 978-1-108-79669-9 Paperback
ISSN 2397-9496 (online)
ISSN 2514-3786 (print)

Christianity and Violence

Elements in Religion and Violence

DOI: 10.1017/9781108859271
First published online: April 2021

Lloyd Steffen
Lehigh University

Author for correspondence: Lloyd Steffen, LHS1@lehigh.edu

ABSTRACT: How Christian people have framed the meaning of violence within their faith tradition has been a complex process subject to all manner of historical, cultural, political, ethnic and theological contingencies. As a tradition encompassing widely divergent beliefs and perspectives, Christianity has, over two millennia, adapted to changing cultural and historical circumstances. To grasp the complexity of this tradition and its involvement with violence requires attention to specific elements explored in this Element: the scriptural and institutional sources for violence; the faith commitments and practices that join communities and sanction both resistance to and authorization for violence; and select historical developments that altered the power wielded by Christianity in society, culture and politics. Relevant issues in social psychology and the moral action guides addressing violence affirmed in Christian communities provide a deeper explanation for the motivations that have led to the diverse interpretations of violence avowed in the Christian tradition.

KEYWORDS: Christians and violence, anti-Jewishness, insecurity, identity protection, white supremacy

ISBNs: 9781108796699 (PB), 9781108859271 (OC)
ISSNs: 2397-9496 (online), 2514-3786 (print)

Contents

1 Religion and Violence: Introduction, Clarifications and Limitations

This contribution to the Cambridge University Press Element series claims to offer insight into the relationship between Christianity and violence. On this topic, even the most cursory review of the faith tradition would support the proposition that violence has been a permanent and ongoing issue since Christianity began over two thousand years ago. In that history, Christians have perpetrated violence through Crusades, heresy trials, anti-Jewish pogroms and anti-Muslim attitudes, the subordination of women, and racist colonialism; they have also been victims of violence. The Religious News Service has reported that "Christians remain one of the most persecuted religious groups in the world ... [with Christians facing] imprisonment, loss of home and assets, torture, rape and even death as a result of their faith."[1] Christians have been proponents and opponents of violence – so what is new to say? How do we go about seeking insight into the relation of Christianity to violence that offers something more than the unremarkable observation that the two notions are of course inextricably intertwined?

This Element is intended to respond to this question. The effort here is not to offer something entirely new and never before seen but to organize an approach to the question about Christianity's relation to violence in such a way that the topic is illuminated. To that end, we must begin by noting some qualifications that are necessary to establish the scope and parameters of this study. Some of these qualifications are themselves obvious things to note about Christianity or violence or the relation between the two, but they are noted because they will provide needed guidance for what will appear in the upcoming pages.

Qualification 1. Christianity is a complex and multiform religion. There are three Christianities, not one – Catholicism, Orthodoxy and Protestantism –

Religious News Service Press Release, "Violence against Christians Surges Globally, Data Shows More than 9K Attacks on Churches in 2019," *Religious News Service*, January 15, 2020, https://religionnews.com/2020/01/15/vio lence-against-christians-surges-globally-data-shows-more-than-9k-attacks-on-churches-in-2019/.

and a variety of forms of Christian faith are encompassed within each of those divisions. (There have been some estimates that as many as 30,000 different forms of Protestantism exist, which is most likely a high exaggeration, but it does make the point.) So, to raise a question about the relation of violence to Christianity requires that one not generalize any particular claim to all structural forms and institutions of Christian identity and certainly not to all Christians. A question, easily overlooked and often suppressed, accompanies this inquiry: When one talks about Christianity and violence to which Christianity – to which institutional form, to which division, to which authorities or Christian identities – is one referring? There will be no one understanding of violence among Christians, no single and unified response to violence on behalf of the faith by faith leaders or even communities, and no single viewpoint on how and whether the faith tradition offers resources to justify violence. Inquiry into the topic of Christianity and violence is a particular way of inquiring into the broader topic of "religion and violence," but "religion" and "violence" are both disputed terms. For present purposes, acknowledging Christianity as a religion is not controversial whatever qualifications one might make to the term "religion." Violence is related to terms like "power" and "force," but since there can be legitimated uses of force that do not amount to violence, this volume will consider violence to be an excessive use of force that causes destruction and harm and especially the injustice of injury. Context often determines how invoking the term "violence" to describe a destructive natural event like a tornado differs from the violence of psychological abuse or physical torture – these different meanings are all legitimate ordinary language uses of the term, but in this Element we shall keep the term violence as it attaches to Christianity to mean that human agency is involved in action, usually intentional, to inflict injury on others.[2]

Qualification 2. A temptation exists to interpret the faith tradition of Christianity as itself providing a source and sanction for acts of violence

---

[2] John D. Carlson, "Religion and Violence: Coming to Terms with Terms," in Andrew R. Murphy, ed., *Blackwell Companion to Religion and Violence* (West Sussex, UK: Wiley Blackwell, 2011): 14–18.

(or, contrariwise, resistance to acts of violence), and care is required on this point. While there is no doubt that Christian beliefs and practices help create bonds of unity to motivate Christian persons to acts that either justify violence or nonviolence under Christian rubrics and action guides, it is not the religion of Christianity writ large that is the actor on the stage of history. Christianity can be, and often is, invoked as if the religion itself were an agent, as if the religion itself were the cause of violence or the actor deciding between action options. But we must beware. Christianity is a cultural institution, a symbol system organized around the ultimate values of religion, but it cannot claim agency. It can affect and does affect decision-making due to the values and action guides that it houses in its various institutional forms, but it is not itself an agent.[3] The problem that arises is that ascribing actor status to a non-agent is to "misplace concreteness," as the informal fallacy by that name asserts. We must beware the *fallacy of reification*, by which is meant that fallacy of ascribing to institutions and nonactor entities the status of actors. An institution, even a cultural institution like a form of a religion, despite being created and perpetuated by human beings, does not as an institution do what real human beings do. Only people are agents. Only people are actors who are motivated to act. Only people are capable of conceiving options for action in the complexity of community life where different ideas, ideologies and institutional frameworks can play a role in providing justification for acting one way rather than another. Reinhold Niebuhr supported the Vietnam war, Martin Luther King opposed it – these two notable twentieth-century Christians found grounding for their perspectives in the Christian tradition, but the

---

[3] In the American legal context, certain institutions – especially companies and corporations acting as non-human persons – have been authorized to enter into contracts, sue and be sued. As fictionalized persons they can be viewed as agents. Such non-human but legal persons, however, do not generate intentionality out of their own resource and are not self-directing agents. Rather, they have agency conferred upon them by human agents acting through legal mechanisms. In that conferral of fictionalized personhood, agency still rests with those who confer agency and claim authorization to do so. Agency, then, in the strict sense of agent-as-person, continues to rest with human rather than non-human persons.

viewpoints advanced and the actions advocated were those of agents who believed their religion had a role to play in deciding policy, direction and action. They invoked what they believed were the action guides that Christianity supported. But these were individual persons – agents – who acted and urged others to do so, not the religion. We must not ascribe agency to Christianity as if it were itself an autonomous agent capable of action and decision-making apart from the people who act based on the values and beliefs and practices they find in their understanding of Christian life and Christian values. Seeking to conform actions to that understanding, people of faith in various ways and in accordance with their commitments of faith will find religion a means that helps frame the values and commitments that affect what they will decide to do to. But human agents do this, not the cultural institution of religion.

Qualification 3. This Element is entitled *Christianity and Violence* rather than *Christian Violence*. Scholars, most notably William Cavanaugh, have questioned the whole idea of "religious violence," his argument being that serious issues arise with how the term religion itself is defined – and most religion scholars do hesitate to define the term. His argument is that in the complicated history in the West, the rise of secularism allowed religion to be cast as fanatical and unreasoning – hence prone to violence – as the state and the push toward secularism created the idea of rational secular violence over against irrational "religious violence."[4] Religious violence is for Cavanaugh a myth designed to bolster the standing of secular authority and justify a secular claim on powers over life and death, including the power of justified state-sponsored violence. The claim to a secular foundation for these powers arose at the expense of religion, which was then, from the viewpoint of rational secularity, relegated to the arena of irrationality, fanaticism and absolutism. From this secular creation of a form of violence contained within the confines of religion – religious violence – a form of violence, a unique form, emerged expressing that irrationality connected to religion – religious violence. This is one view – that religious violence is

---

[4] William Cavanaugh, *The Myth of Religious Violence: Secular Ideology and the Roots of Modern Conflict* (Oxford: Oxford University Press, 2009).

a myth. There are other scholars who support the idea that there is something inherent in religious ideas that lends credence to the idea of religious violence – this would include, in quite different ways, Richard Wentz, John Hick, Charles Kimball, Mark Juergensmeyer, even Martin Marty and his claim that religion is divisive – so whether there is such a thing as religious violence is a scholar's debate in many respects. This study does not take a decisive stand on the issue, but it does believe that the idea of "religion and violence" avoids some implications of causality provoked by 'religious violence' and keeps the concepts of religion and violence conceptually distinct so that the relationship between the two can be more carefully examined. "Religion and violence" allows that that casual observation previously mentioned – that of course Christianity seems to have been involved with violence – now lays before us to be explored.

Qualification 4. Although what lies ahead will lead us into Christianity's sacred scriptures[5] and into history and even some psychology explorations, the topic of religion and violence is essentially fodder for ethics. This is because violence is human action decided upon by human beings and anything human beings do and decide to do is subject to moral analysis. Although institutions within Christianity, like Church bodies, may play a significant role in gathering people to address violence, for or against, the responsibility for Christians acting violently or choosing to oppose violence lies with the people who are, as agents, making decisions to express their religiosity – their faith – one way in preference to another with respect to the question of violence.

Qualification 5. Violence involving religion can have special characteristics, just as one might find distinctive characteristics with violence as it arises politically, economically, ethnically, racially, or in response to a phenomenon like globalization. But religion does demand careful scrutiny. Matthew Isaac cites research that conflicts involving religion are more violent than other forms of conflict; that violence involving religion is more violent and longer lasting than other forms of violence"; and that

The New Revised Standard Version of the Bible (NRSV) has been used throughout.

"While some scholars maintain that religious beliefs encourage violence, there is also reason to believe that violence encourages religion."[6] (The rhetoric of religion, Isaac argues, can serve to mobilize people in their social and political conflicts, religion providing a strong foundation for social solidarity in the face of conflict.)

While these preliminary qualifications have been brought forward to frame the inquiry that follows, this investigation into the "elements" of "Christianity and Violence" involves several other factors that will provide a focus for discussions to follow. These foci are relevant to ethics and moral psychology, for always at issue when violence comes into the picture is why the option for violence is chosen as a good and viable option, which must be assumed since it was in fact chosen, and it is reasonable to assume people choose what they believe to be good rather than bad options.

An overarching issue pertains to locating this study, as mentioned, in the arena of ethical analysis and moral psychology. The question of violence always concerns itself with motive, taken here to mean a backward-looking reason for action, and intention, taken here to be a forward-looking reason for action. What is the motive for violence undertaken by Christian people in the course of the conflicts they have endured throughout history? What intentions are in play when Christians encounter violence? Accompanying the motive–intention issue, Christian people involved with violence will take a stand in relation to violence due to the several relevant factors, including the following, which will specify "elements" relevant to the discussion about the relationship of Christianity to violence:

1. *Insecurity*. Clearly, one motive for the Christian resorting to violence is the profound experience of insecurity and vulnerability.

[6] Matthew Isaac, "Sacred Violence or Strategic Faith? Disentangling the Relationship between Religion and Violence in Armed Conflict," *Journal of Peace Research*, Vol. 53, no. 2 (February 2016): 211.https://doi.org/10.1177/0022343315626771. Worthy of note is the research of Joshua D. Wright, "More Religion, Less Justification for Violence: A Cross-National Analysis," *Archive for the Psychology of Religion*, Vol. 38, no. 2 (2016): 159–183. Wright argues that the more religious persons are around such beliefs as life-after-death, the less likely they are to be perpetrators of violence.

2. *Dialectic of violence and nonviolence.* Referencing once again the diversity of viewpoints within the wide bailiwick of the world's largest religion, Christianity, it is important to recognize the diversity of beliefs and practices and think about them in terms of a dialectic. Of course certain affirmations of faith will appear universal to Christians, the importance and centrality of Jesus of Nazareth and the New Testament Scriptures, for instance, but still the details of the many denominations and divisions within the faith tradition point to differences in content, emphasis, belief and practice. Since there is no one religious viewpoint on the question of how to understand violence from a Christian perspective, discussions of justification for violence will often be met by other Christians opposing violence also on religious grounds. The violence/nonviolence dialectic will be a constant issue in this volume.

3. *Punishment and identity.* Another motive for resorting to violence is to inflict punishment for actions deemed threatening to good or established order or to the faith community's commitments of doctrine and practice. Violence is a way to respond to challenges to identity – and the future identity – of Christian persons and their communities (Church), which provides the structure for identity and its continuity generation to generation. The preservation of identity through punishment, the fear of losing identity and the desire to enforce identity on others, have all been motivations for violence.

4. *Protection of identity.* The use of violence to protect identity points to practices that may violate moral norms, but which also indicate, even if quite backhandedly, pursuit of the end of securing peace and social harmony. Violence is, curiously, a means of conflict resolution when the community or the faith identity is threatened. Resorting to violence can indicate support for practices that demean people on the basis of race, sex or gender, or subject innocent persons to threats of harm through terrorist activities, yet such violence can be interpreted in ways that demonstrate aspirations to peace through religiously affirmed values for the religious community. Specifically, Christian people who resort to violence may seek to conform their actions to what is believed to be the divine will in particular conflicts. Violence can be justified as a means –

unfortunate perhaps – to move through conflict because the end that is sought is peace and social harmony for the community of faith.

Looking ahead, we shall begin by examining the sources of Christian affirmation in the early theological work of St. Paul and in the life of Jesus of Nazareth as told by the Gospels. We shall then examine various instances of violence in the history of the West where Christianity has made a response by justifying violence or refusing to justify it; then, in a third section, conclude with an examination of the ways in which Christian identity is an issue relevant to violence, examining issues such as war, punishment, inquisition, heresy and even Christian terrorism.

2 Theological Sources and Sanctions for Violence and Nonviolence

Violence has played a significant role in the history – and in the internal story – of Christianity from its very beginning. The birth narratives of Jesus in the New Testament, for instance, one obvious starting point in the Christian story, announce through heavenly heralds an explicit message of peace on earth and good will to all people. That message of peace suppresses a more subtle story of violence. Even the Christmas story manifests the element of violence–nonviolence since the parents-to-be at the center of the story were on the road to Bethlehem, traditional site of Jesus' birth, because of an obligation to obey an imperial census decree. Thus, the story provides a reminder that the world into which Jesus was born was marked by military occupation. The occupier, Rome, remains, even in today's memory, one of the most violent and brutal imperial regimes the world has ever known, and that reputation is hardly ameliorated by the roads, aqueducts and all the other Roman engineering marvels.

First century Israel-Palestine was properly known as Judea, a Roman territory that identified both the area around Jerusalem as well as the wider area of Palestine inhabited by Jews. Jerusalem was the center of the world for Jews, for the Temple where God dwelt was to be found in this ancient city, which had long been a site of annual pilgrimage. When Jesus was born Palestine was ruled by a ruthless Roman vassal, Herod the Great, the son of whom, upon his death, would divide power and unsuccessfully govern Galilee, Judea and Samaria. So much unrest ensued that Rome appointed a Roman governor, Pontius Pilate, to assert Rome's hard hand of discipline on the land, and Roman authority was strongly in place as the story of Jesus unfolds in the Gospel stories.

The years of the first century were socially unstable, politically conflicted and economically oppressive. Heavy tax burdens imposed on farmers led rural inhabitants in the wider area to migrate to urban centers, and discontent only grew in urban settings. The Romans were hated by the local populations, and the political skirmishes and revolts against Rome would finally culminate in the 66 CE Jewish War. Rome would suppress rebellions arising from a dissatisfied and resentful indigenous population; and religion was not unaffected by all the turmoil.[7] Messianism, apocalypticism and Zealotry had become major ideological attachments for religious people in Judea in the two centuries leading up to Jesus' birth, and the Roman war against the Jews would finally lead to the destruction of the Jerusalem Temple in 70 CE.

The razing of the Temple, this dwelling place of the Holy One, proved to be a singular moment in the history of the religious life of Jews and of Christians as well. Jews did not find in the Jewish sect of Christianity reason to adopt the Christian belief that messianic hopes had been realized in the person and work of Jesus as the Christ; and the destruction of the Temple further separated Christians from Jews, reflecting an anti-temple theme that is quite pronounced in the Gospels where it is even attributed to Jesus himself. The early first century history of Christianity is noteworthy for the conflicts of the early Christians with Jews and the Jewish community, with Roman authorities, and with parties internal to Christianity itself. In dealing with those conflicts, Christians turned to source authorities to discern what to believe and how to act, and the writings of Paul and the story of the life of Jesus would prove to be determinative for Christians seeking to discern the will of the divine. These authorities would be consulted on the issue of violence and whether and how it can be sanctioned and justified as consistent with – if not exactly integral to – the tenets of faith. The role that violence played in the development of the religion of Christianity can been seen even in brief compass by examining relevant aspects of Christianity's most important figures in the first century, St. Paul and Jesus of Nazareth.

St. Paul

St. Paul is memorable for a variety of reasons. He was, first of all, a liberal Pharisaic Jew who became a founder of the religion of Christianity after originally opposing all things Christian. As the Book of Acts of the Apostles in the New Testament tells it, he was present at the stoning of Christianity's first noteworthy martyr, Stephen, and approved of the killing (Acts 8.1). So in his first appearances in Scripture, St. Paul – originally Saul of Tarsus – is identified as an opponent of Christianity sanctioning a lethal act of violence. Moreover, Paul, prior to his adoption of the new faith, is known, according to the author of Acts, as a persecutor of Christians, one who entered by force the homes of Christian men and women, imprisoned them, and "breath(ed) threats and murder against the disciples of the Lord" (Acts 9.1). But Saul does accept Christian faith claims, and, as one who would share with the original disciples the title of "Apostle," also understands that the demand of the new religion is for a missionary proselytizing faith that seeks to make converts. While not inherently violent, such a mission for the faith could lend itself to coercion and violence, and subsequent missionary history would bear out that this did in fact happen and with some frequency. The Book of Acts also shares that Paul and St. Peter divided the outreach mission of the new faith between them, Peter continuing to spread the Gospel message to Jews, and Paul taking the message to Gentiles or non-Jews. It is this mission to the non-Jewish world that allows us to say of St. Paul that he is responsible for envisioning a wider post-Jewish vision of Christianity. Paul's missionary activity, along with that vision of outreach to the Gentile world, is what contributed more than anything else in the history of the faith tradition to making Christianity a world religion.

Paul's letters, the earliest writings in the New Testament, are addressed to the church communities he helped found, Rome being an already-established exception. In his letters, Paul settles conflicts that have arisen internal to the churches and makes a theological appeal to those ideas that reinforce commitment and identity and establish social harmony for the faith communities. Paul lays out the major theological concepts that will provide the scaffolding of ideas that will then identify the tenets of faith for Christians. It is in developing this scaffolding that Paul becomes the true founder of the religion of Christianity. He provides the explanation conceptually for what the "Christ event" means even if he pays almost no attention to anything having to do with the actual life of Jesus of Nazareth. Emphasizing God's grace, justification by faith and the sacramental unity of Christians through baptism and eucharist (communion), Paul establishes the core affirmations around which Christian faith and community life will develop, including human equality before God, freedom from Jewish legal constraints, an eschatological hope for Christ's return, and his "justification by faith" notion that by faith in Christ's salvific work humanity had been, in history, reconciled with God.

But even in this theological explication so important to Christian identity, violence makes an appearance, and Paul will address issues of violence and examine them in light of the faith tradition. A major Pauline emphasis is on atonement, the idea that the Christ was a sacrifice that reconciled a fallen and sinful humanity with a God of grace whose sense of justice required that the standing of humanity be justified for a relationship with God. Important to this idea of atonement – this making of 'at-one-ment' – is the idea of a sacrifice pleasing to God's justice which then effects a reconciliation between God and humanity through that sacrifice. As modeled in the Torah: "For the life of the flesh is in the blood; and I have given it to you for making atonement for your lives on the altar; for, as life, it is the blood that makes the atonement" (Leviticus 17.11). Christ's suffering and death on the cross provided the blood for the atonement St. Paul made central to Christian theology.

Of importance in examining Paul's theology is the primary fact that the Hebrew religion by ancient tradition was very much an altar religion that provided Paul with a template for his Christian theology. The Temple in Jerusalem was the site of Jewish sacrifice and the story in the Gospels of Jesus chasing the money changers out of the temple was very much tied to the sale of animals for sacrifice, especially lambs and baby goats for

Passover. Those sacrificial acts would provide blood for dousing the altar, effecting reconciliation between penitent and God, and ritualistically cleansing persons and allowing them to receive forgiveness for their sins from God. Additionally, the roasting of the meat from animal sacrifices was thought to present a pleasing aroma to God, and it announced sinful humanity's desire to seek forgiveness for sin: "The priest shall dash the blood against the altar of the Lord at the entrance of the tent of meeting, and turn the fat into smoke as a pleasing odor to the Lord" (Leviticus 17.6). Roman Catholicism, incidentally, is also in many respects an altar religion, for the Mass is a reenactment of Christ's sacrifice, an acknowledgment of body and blood offered at the altar site to God on behalf of penitent sinners, and the ritualistic saturating of the altar with incense even recalls the aroma feature of ancient sacrifice.

With the ancient Hebrew tradition of sacrificing an innocent and pure animal to provide propitiation to God, the burnt sacrifice of an innocent animal, which was then consumed after roasting, allowed for the reestablishment of a proper relationship between God and those making the sacrifice. This understanding of ritual sacrifice of an innocent animal as the ritual God accepted for forgiveness of sin provided Paul with the basic template of his atonement theology. In this ultimate act of atonement, Christ takes on humanity's sin and presents to God the act of propitiation that satisfies the divine will and reconciles God to humanity. The sacrifice of an innocent – Jesus, often referred to as the "lamb" of God – provides the salvific event that enables God's justice vis-à-vis sinful humanity to establish a right – or justified – relationship between God and humanity. So Christ's atoning work repairs the relationship between God and humanity broken by sin, and it is due to Christ's willing sacrificial death on the cross, a death God required but Christ needed to accept willingly, now after Calvary takes on the staggering importance of a once-for-all sacrifice that never need be repeated. Christ as an innocent took on the sin of humanity, and as a result God and humanity are permanently reconciled, the cross being the symbol for that reconciliation. Jesus' death then is not in Pauline theology remembered as a political execution but a meta-theological symbol whereby Jesus as the Christ served the divine will and effected a reconciling of humanity with God.

This atonement theology is commonplace theology in most forms of Christianity, so much so that the violence is overlooked. At the heart of this atonement theology is the idea that the intended and willful death of an innocent person as a means to a divinely willed end – a prima facie wrong – could be willed by God, who in most theologies does not act unjustly or do wrong. Atonement theology in Christianity invites speculation on a divine violence against an innocent, an updating in some respects of the story of Job in the Hebrew Wisdom literature. Actually, Muslim theologians have been much more open to delving into the meaning of the atonement theology, some to the point of criticizing the idea that God could will an unjust act. Some leading Muslim theologians have thus argued that Jesus did not really die on the cross, because that would posit wrongdoing in the divine will itself. Something tricky – illusory – happened: Simon of Cyrene who carried Jesus' cross to the execution site took on Jesus' appearance and died in his place, or perhaps Jesus' body was not a physical body but a spiritual form unaffected by the violence of the crucifixion. The purpose of such speculations was to avoid implicating God in an act of injustice, namely, the wrongful death of an innocent man. The justice issue internal to God aside, there is no question that this atonement theology is violent – that it demands a human sacrifice.

Paul's writings have a decided ethical emphasis. They charge the faithful to love another, extend hospitality to the stranger, live in harmonious community, bless one's persecutors and overcome evil with good. Paul addresses many issues related to ethics and right conduct, and he addressed in his ethical reflections issues related to government legitimacy. His ethical injunctions will be consulted for guidance throughout the history of the Christian faith, and the reflections on government have been important for providing Christians with justifications for state-sponsored violence. Paul himself does not appeal to any coercive force in response to his personal sufferings or persecutions of others in the early church, but he does develop ideas about government, discusses uses of force Christians can accept as legitimate and sanctioned by God, and he even attends to some specifics as to what the Christian owes the state:

> Let every person be subject to the governing authorities; for
> there is no authority except from God, and those authorities

that exist have been instituted by God. Therefore whoever resists authority resists what God has appointed, and those who resist will incur judgement. For rulers are not a terror to good conduct but to bad . . . if you do wrong you should be afraid, for the authority does not bear the sword in vain! It is the servant of God to execute wrath upon the wrong-doer. Therefore one must be subject, not only because of wrath but because of conscience. For the same reason you are also to pay taxes, for the authorities are God's servants. (Romans 13.1–7a).

The image of importance in this passage is the "sword" wielded by the state. Paul seems to legitimate the power of the sword as an instrument of the state's coercive power, which can include a power over life and death. Paul's appeal in the Romans passage is to Christians, and the appeal is not to coercive power but to conscience – all power over life and death comes from God and Christians are to adhere to that principle. The state has things it must do – such as collect taxes and punish those who violate the law out of bad conduct – but St. Paul does not explicitly endorse violence. John Howard Yoder has argued that there is "a very strong strand of Gospel teaching which sees secular government as the province of the sovereignty of Satan."[8] For Yoder, government functions given God's oversight of governmental power do not go beyond ordering society under law and regulations, and the idea is that governmental ordering is much akin to the way libraries order all the materials that they must classify and catalogue so that the materials can be of practical use. For Yoder, the ordering function does not legitimate any use of violence – Yoder was a pacifist Mennonite – and coercive force receives no divine sanction. State violence is anti-Christian, the work of Satan (anti-Christ) and antithetical to the Christian message of peace and love.

Yet this acknowledgment in Paul of the power of the "sword" has led many Christians over the centuries to appeal to Paul as one who provided

---

[8] John Howard Yoder, The *Politics of Jesus* (Grand Rapids, MI: Eerdmans, 1972) 195.

legitimation for governmental power and even the state power to kill. The governmental power of the sword on this view extends God's will into the secular world on God's behalf, including an execution power. One does have to ask of those who support state-sponsored executions by appeal to these Pauline verses if it is credible to think that in the Letter to the Romans, where Paul is imprisoned and himself awaiting execution, he is actually spending his writing time justifying Rome in its hold on such a power while articulating a divine sanction for his own state-sponsored killing. Nevertheless, Romans 13.1–7a does lend credibility to the view that there is Christian warrant in Paul for governments to use coercion and force. A Christian appeal to Paul to legitimate and sanction violence as consistent with the divine will is a justification that will later be taken up by the Church as a governing authority as it claims power to direct coercion against heretics or other perceived enemies of the Church, thereby undermining of the social harmony sought through Church governance.

Jesus/Christ

There is no person in history about whom so much has been written and so little known for certain than Jesus of Nazareth. Jesus, the centerpiece of Christian belief and practice, is obscure to history though there is no doubt there was such a person; and his impact on history and culture is unparalleled. (Although it is no indisputable proof of the historical existence of Jesus, the Roman historians Tacitus, Pliny and Suetonius all mention Christians and its founder in their respective histories.) St. Paul did not know Jesus and in his writing says almost nothing about the "historical Jesus." This was due to Paul's eschatological belief that Jesus, risen as the Christ and ascended to heaven, was going to come again in a final judgment; and in Paul's earliest letter, 1 Thessalonians, it is clear that he expected that return soon. Early Christians were very much caught up in the expectation of the immediacy of Christ's return and greeted one another with the word "Maranatha" – "our Lord cometh." Detailing events Paul might have known about Jesus' life were not relevant material for inclusion in his letters, especially when Jesus' followers would have presumably known the same stories, and for Paul the importance of Jesus was his status as the resurrected "Christ" (Greek for "messiah") who fulfilled the expectation

Jews had held of a redeemer and liberator who would create a new basis for relationship with God. Jesus' death on the cross was central to Paul's theology of atonement, and it rested on an historical fact – that Jesus was executed by the Romans. That death was also the precondition for resurrection, which signaled Christ's redemption of humankind.

What is known about the life and teachings of Jesus of Nazareth comes mainly from early Christian writings, especially the Gospels of the New Testament. In those texts, Jesus appears as a teacher and preacher. He taught in parables, according to the Gospels, which were stories from everyday life situations that were probably open-ended in their original telling. They dealt with religion, obviously, but also, more subversively, they addressed politics and economics as well. As a preacher, Jesus' message was to announce within the hearing of those to whom he spoke the coming of the Kingdom of God. That Kingdom was open to those who loved their enemies, returned good for evil and lived under a divine command to love God and their neighbor. He was also known as a healer, and his teaching and preaching attracted a large and loyal following, though in at least one parable, that of the Talents (Matthew 25:14–30), his story seems to be praising those who risk capital and get a high return on wisely-placed financial investments.

Jesus emphasized reconciliation, forgiveness and an equitable sharing among his followers. In his preaching and parable-focused teaching Jesus opposed violence, vengeance, hatred, retaliation and even retribution. A gospel story shows him interfering with what may have been a lawful execution under Hebrew law – the stoning of an adulteress; and when pressed about the role of government he cryptically advocated that one "render unto Caesar what was Caesar's" (Matthew 12.17) and unto God what was God's – and it is all God's, though this was not said. Jesus was no political philosopher nor even an ethicist and he did not endorse any "power of the sword" except to say in opposition to sword-related violence that "all who take the sword will perish by the sword" (Matthew 26.52). Jesus did not condemn those who served the state as soldiers or tax collectors – he praised the faith of a Roman centurion (Matthew 8.13) and he called into his fellowship of twelve disciples Matthew, who is identified in the Gospels as a tax collector (Matthew 10.3).

Jesus appears in the Gospels to be a pacifist – he goes so far as to say "resist not evil" (Matthew 5.38) in the Sermon on the Mount. (The Sermon on the Plane, another version of this most famous of Jesus' teaching, is found in Luke 6.20–49). The idea of doing nothing to resist an evildoer identifies an extreme form of pacifism that would inspire Leo Tolstoy's absolutist philosophy of non-resistance.

Violence, however, is not far from some of Jesus' words and actions; and, if Jesus is an advocate of nonviolence, he is a less-than-absolutist pacifist, as can be gleaned from certain details to be found in the Gospel narratives. Attributed to him are the words, "I did not come to bring peace but a sword," (Matthew 10.34), and he seems to incite conflict when he utters in Matthew 10. 35a, "I have come to set a man against his father, and a daughter against her mother." Open to many different interpretations, these hard sayings make it difficult to escape the conclusion that Jesus' message is doing more than pointing to a consequence of discipleship. These words may actually articulate a part of his mission.

The story of Jesus cleansing the Jerusalem temple of money changers and those selling goods and animals for sacrifice comes closer to seeing an angry Jesus actually engaged in violence. The Gospel of John adds that Jesus used "whips of cord" to cleanse the temple of animals and money changers (John 2.15), an act of righteous indignation perhaps but still a resorting to violence. He struck the money changers so that one might assume a desire on his part to inflict harm or punishment on those who violated the holy space of the Jerusalem temple, which, as previously noted, was for Jews the holiest place on earth. If "violence" is too strong a term to describe Jesus' action in the Temple cleansing, one can at least note that Jesus did not negotiate, invite mediation or opt for other nonviolent strategies but went directly to coercive force to achieve his end, which was to preserve the ritual purity of the Temple space and the Holy of Holies.

Of course, the central event in the Jesus story – so critical for the atonement theology of Paul – was Jesus' crucifixion. Early Christians were upset that many Jews had not converted to the new faith, and this upset found its way into the Gospel narratives. Jews are presented as the instigators of the events leading up to Jesus' death, even claiming that Jesus

had been tried before a night-time session of the Sanhedrin, which condemned Jesus for blasphemy, but which as a matter of history never – ever –
met at night according to the Mishnah. Jews are shown in Pilate's presentation of Jesus to the crowd in Jerusalem just prior to the crucifixion as calling
for Jesus blood to fall on them if guilt for this impending death needs to fall
somewhere: "His blood be upon us and our children "(Matthew 27.25).

For Christian readers of these texts, the blood guilt was removed from
Rome and placed on the Jews who are shown calling for Jesus' death, but
nothing obscures the fact that Rome executed Jesus, and Rome found reason
to execute him. The condemnation from Roman authority via Pontius Pilate
is common to all the Gospels and there is no reason to suspect that Jesus'
death was anything but a typical dispensing of Roman justice as it was applied
against those deemed an enemy of the state – and Jesus dies the death of an
enemy of Rome. His crime? Sedition. If the Kingdom of God Jesus preached
was truly a vision of a new and different life free of violence and state terror,
then it is worth noting that Jesus did oppose Rome and its values and was
indeed guilty of sedition vis-à-vis the Roman status quo.[9] And the punishment dispensed by Rome was cruel and agonizingly violent. The crucifixion
as an act of violence is what propels the historical Jesus toward a death that
ends not in the grave but as a central tenet of Christian faith, namely, belief in
the resurrection which occurs two days later. That belief in resurrection is
what allows a risen Christ to claim victory over death, death being the
consequences of sin, and sin being the term that identifies not moral wrongdoing but disrelationship with God. In the atonement theology so central to
Paul and to most forms of orthodox Christianity, Christ's resurrection
represents the power of God to conquer death with life and the promise of
life everlasting to those who believe in the power of God to resurrect Jesus as
the Christ, for resurrection removed barriers to a proper, acceptable and
"justified" relationship between God and humanity. Resurrection was the
ultimate affirmation that the sacrifice Jesus offered – his own life – was
acceptable to God and redemptive for humanity. The consequence of sin –
death – had been overcome by raising Jesus in glory. And in glory Jesus

[9] I emphasize this point in a discussion in Lloyd Steffen, *Executing Justice: The
Moral Meaning of the Death Penalty* (Eugene, OR: Wipf & Stock, 2006).

would return – that being the eschatological hope so important to early Christians.

Jesus may or may not have been a pacifist, but what is clear is that in the early years of the faith, Christians who did not observe the formalities of Roman religious obligation were perceived as enemies of the state, and speculation has often fallen on the idea that the presentation of Jesus as a pacifist in the Gospels was, among other things, meant to give testimony to the fact that early Christians were no threat to the Roman empire. Nero's persecutions of Christians also provided the authorities with a convenient scapegoat for events like the Great Fire in Rome. A widely held speculation is that the fire had been started by Nero himself, but Nero blamed and then persecuted Christians for the Great Fire.[10]

Christians were clearly victims of persecution, but they were also perpetrators of bigotry and hatred toward Jews. The violence/nonviolence dialectic is clearly at work in any examination of the early church texts and history, and the persecution of Christians by the Roman authorities must be viewed as one story of violence during this period, but not the only one. The New Testament and the Gospel stories in particular are marred by a hard thump of anti-Jewishness as Jews were blamed for entering into a conspiracy with Rome to bring about Jesus' death. The consequences of this claim affirmed by Christians down through the centuries in Europe gave rise to terrible acts of slaughter against the Jews, the resultant anti-

[10] Tacitus wrote in the *Annals*: "Therefore, to stop the rumor [that he had set Rome on fire], he [Emperor Nero] falsely charged with guilt, and punished with the most fearful tortures, the persons commonly called Christians, who were [generally] hated for their enormities. Christus, the founder of that name, was put to death as a criminal by Pontius Pilate, procurator of Judea, in the reign of Tiberius, but the pernicious superstition – repressed for a time, broke out yet again, not only through Judea, – where the mischief originated, but through the city of Rome also, whither all things horrible and disgraceful flow from all quarters, as to a common receptacle, and where they are encouraged. Accordingly first those were arrested who confessed they were Christians; next on their information, a vast multitude were convicted not so much on the charge of burning the city, as of 'hating the human race.'" Eyewitness to History.com, "Nero Persecutes Christians 64 A.D.," www.eyewitnesstohistory.com/christians.htm.

Jewishness so endemic to Western culture culminating in the Holocaust of the Second World War. The Gospels are replete with anti-Jewish attitudes and messages,[11] so much so that contemporary services in many more liberal Christian churches go out of their way to avoid sharing Scripture readings during the Lenten season of the Church calendar if the passages articulate this anti-Jewishness. Some Christians, then, actually censor Christianity's sacred scriptures to counter a sad history of anti-Jewishness pervasive in the tradition and conform the Jesus narrative with contemporary demands for historical accuracy and more enlightened moral attitudes.

Jesus is said to have asked his disciples, "Who do you say that I am?" (Matthew 16.15) and the historical record points to disagreements within that huge gathering of believers who identified as Christians. Disputes over the identity of Jesus Christ and how he was to be understood as human and divine and as part of a trinitarian Godhead, were profound, and those disagreements would themselves give rise to serious conflicts leading to lethal violence. Disputes about the identity of Christ – was he human or divine, or both? – led to the shedding of blood and attempts to impose an "orthodoxy" on the question. Councils like those at Nicaea and Chalcedon resolved disputes and created orthodox theological doctrine on questions pertaining to the nature of God and the nature of Christ, for at stake were the community's affirmation of those right beliefs that were tied up with the Christian promise of salvation and a promise of life beyond this world:

> The vast majority of people at this time, educated and ignorant, believed in providential views of the world. They believed that wrong conduct or heretical belief stirred God to anger, and that such anger would be expressed in highly material terms, in earthquakes and fire, invasion and military defeat, famine and pestilence.[12]

[11] Samuel Sandmel, *Anti-Semitism in the New Testament* (Philadelphia: Fortress, 1978).

[12] Philip Jenkins, *Jesus Wars : How Four Patriarchs, Three Queens, and Two Emperors Decided What Christians Would Believe for the Next 1,5000 Years* (New York: HarperOne, 2011), 26.

Much was at stake in individual Christian lives and in their communities as they concerned themselves with right conduct and right belief, which provided the foundation for establishing social harmony and affirming an identity as right-believing Christians. To be Christian was to be beset with a very literal "fear of God," along with fear of those enemies, which included other Christians internally and external enemies, like Nero, who persecuted those in the faith. As much as early Christians may have experienced insecurity in the face of such challenges, they also showed they were quite capable of responding to such insecurity by focusing energy on forging the bonds of unity necessary for identity in their faith communities. The history of the early church demonstrates that they would apply themselves energetically, assiduously and at times even fanatically to the construction of these identities, often, as we shall see later, by resorting to violence.

Looking Ahead

The history of the early Christian Church is enormously complex but a couple of events are worth noting. The most significant historical accident to befall Christianity, which Christians at the time believed was God-willed, was the conversion of the Emperor Constantine to Christianity in 312. This followed a victory over the Eastern Emperor Lucinius. Having consolidated power, Constantine became sole Emperor, and the year this occurred, 324, is regarded as the beginning of the Christian Empire. The historian of Christianity Jean Comby explained the meaning of this momentous event:

> The Kingdom of God had come down to earth. Christians now accepted the sacred nature of the emperor, whom they naturally enough looked to as the head of the Christian people: a new Moses, a new David... The clergy obtained legal privileges: the Episcopal tribunals had a civil jurisdiction, and the bishops were considered to be on an equal footing with governors.[13]

Jean Comby, *How to Read Church History, Vol. I: From the Beginning to the Fifteenth Century* (New York: Crossroads, 1992), 68, 75.

Christianity became the official religion of the Empire by decree of Emperor Theodosius in 380 and thus entered a new age of dealing with power and even adopting, for reason of internal supervision and administration, "the power of the sword." Christianity was not offering a vision distinct from that attached to the power of the secular state at this time; there was no way to distinguish the secular from the sacred with these developments. Christianity integrated with the political machinations of Empire, taking on the role of a major political force that would affect Christianity and Western civilization down to the current day. At the time this happened, rabbinic Judaism and Christianity further distanced themselves from one another and conflicts between the two tradition's intensified. James Carroll has written:

> Christians went from being a private, apolitical movement to being a shaper if world politics. The status of Judaism was similarly reversed, from a licit self-rule a respected exception within a sea of paganism, to a state of highly vulnerable disenfranchisement. What might be called history's first pogrom, an organized assault on a community of Jews, because they were Jews, took place in Alexandria in 414, wiping out that city's Jewish community for a time. Even in Palestine, Jews became a besieged minority.[14]

Garbed with the trappings of imperial power, Christian people came to understand that the new status of their religion was the result of God's will – "God having acted in history" we might say today; and that what this meant vis-à-vis the Jews is that Christians understood that they had come to replace the Jews as God's chosen people. This move theologians describe under the term "supersessionism," and it enabled Christians who wielded imperial power, which included military power, to identify Jews as dethroned from any place of privilege with God with claims otherwise rendering them enemies not only of Christianity but now of the state as well. The logical consequence of this alteration in status was that Jews were

[14] James Carroll, *Constantine's Sword: The Church and the Jews, A History* (New York: Mariner Books, Houghton Mifflin, 2001), 176.

made subject to imperial restrictions. So, for example, an edict in 315 made it a crime for Jews to proselytize; then, a century later, proselytizing by Jews was declared a capital crime. Thus did a religion that in many ways began on Calvary with the execution of a Jewish teacher proclaiming the Kingdom of God wind up imposing thousands of Calvaries on those victimized by the vicissitudes of history and the desire of Christian-state actors to persecute those now denied their historical identity as chosen by God, an identity Jesus as a Jew would in all likelihood have affirmed. And the justification for these moves was that God was obviously working to bring about Christian supremacy in history itself. The rise of Christianity to its place as a supreme religion sanctioned by the imperial state occurred with divine approval, for history was the arena where God was allowing the dynamic increase of Christian power and influence to occur. This understanding granted enormous support to the legitimation of coercive power to maintain the supremacy that was clearly – or so it was believed – God-willed.

3 Insecurity and Vulnerability

Wherever violence is a part of the Christian story, we can find the four elements that play a part in giving rise to – or responding to – violence: insecurity and vulnerability, the dialectic of violence and nonviolence, the issue of punishment and identity stabilization, and actions to protect Christian identity while seeking social harmony. Any element may appear in the foreground while others are backgrounded – how they appear will depend on the way events are recounted and on the way the analysis proceeds. The focus in this section is on the insecurity–vulnerability element, the task here being to discern the role it played as Christian people decided to unleash violence in the world in relation to some specific historical events.

The idea that insecurity is involved in the Christian response to violence begins with an acknowledgment that as much as Christians might think of themselves as spiritual beings, they are also finite beings subject to the natural processes that affect the human body and which lead eventually to physical decline and death, that ultimate and universal marker of finitude. What happens to the body can of course affect how human beings understand themselves spiritually, that is, as beings who are free and not

determined in all respects by natural limitation; and among those factors
that affect natural limitation and thus human well-being – body and spirit –
are such things as weather and climate change, sickness and disease, famine
and hunger, floods and water shortages, earthquakes, landslides, tsunamis
and all manner of events human beings bring about by policy decisions,
inventions, discoveries and interventions in nature. Violence can arise in
reaction to insecurity and the many perceived threats to human well-being,
and insecurity is itself a response to fear.[15]

No doubt the fears generated by finitude are powerful in the lives of
individuals, but at issue are the moments when, in the history of Christianity
and the experience of Christian people, insecurities have generated violence. The example I wish to consider to illustrate this point is the Black
Death in fourteenth-century Europe.

Background

The modern world has known the insecurity of living with plague and
pandemic – the fear of contracting a fatal illness, the anxieties attached to
the possible loss of family and friends, and the disquieting experience of
living in the face of threats to livelihood and the breakdown of social
structures, economic arrangements and political institutions. The Spanish
Flu outbreak during the First World War, which killed upwards of one
hundred million people – a high estimate but only half the number of those
killed by the Black Death of the fourteenth century – visited such

---

[15] "Fear is defined as 'the institutional, cultural and psychological repercussion of
violence' (Kruijt and Koonings, 1999: 15) that produces a sense of 'insecurity' and
vulnerability (Arriagada and Godoy, 2000). Although perceptions of insecurity
are not always borne out by statistical evidence, they fundamentally affect
well-being (Kaplinsky, 2001). 'Livelihood security', denoting the ability to
access resources to ensure survival, is closely interrelated with a series of
structural factors underpinning violence, while citizen insecurity is also closely
linked with a failure of government public security (McIlwaine and Moser,
2003)." From "Working Paper 245: Change, Violence and Insecurity in Non-
Conflict Situations," Caroline O. N. Moser and Dennis Rodgers (London:
Overseas Development Institute, March 2005): 4, www.odi.org/sites/odi.org
.uk/files/odi-assets/publications-opinion-files/1824.pdf.

insecurities on a global scale only a few generations ago. Even more contemporaneously, however, the COVID-19 coronavirus has led to widespread fear and some curious denial reactions that indicate insecurity.

Human beings seek to understand the cause of natural events; this is a universal psychological reality. In fourteenth-century Europe, the explanatory system for how the natural world functioned – and this would encompass the onslaught of disease and pandemic – was religion. Science and its methodologies had not yet become a source of accepted causal explanation despite some initial grounding in the West in Aristotle and other Greek philosophers. In fourteenth-century Europe, religion was the primary source of explanation for natural events, including natural disasters; and if terrible and fear-inducing events were affecting human beings through epidemic or pandemic disease, then the explanation had to be religion-based – for instance, God had been offended by human sin and disease was delivered as divine punishment. It is curious that in the COVID-19 pandemic of 2020 the explanatory system for the disease once again showed itself to be for many people religious or akin to religious – "religious" in the peculiar sense of being "nonscientific." In the twenty-first century coronavirus pandemic in the United States, it is science that has been denied standing as the overarching and unquestioned explanatory system. For many, science itself has been attacked, replaced by an ersatz religion of anti-science as governmental leaders rely on political expediency tied apparently in some cases to egoistic intuition about the course of the disease, that intuition being a nonscientific perspective offered as explanation-diagnosis and expectation-prognosis.[16] Science, which began to displace religion as the explanatory system for understanding the natural world

[16] Adam Wernock, "How Science Denial on the Political Right Hampers the US Response to Covid-19," *The World* (April 22, 2020), www.pri.org/stories/2020-04-22/how-science-denial-political-right-hampers-us-response-covid-19; Adrian Bardon, "Coronavirus Responses Highlight How Humans Have Evolved to Dismiss Facts that Don't Fit Their Worldview," *Scientific American*, The Conversation US (June 26, 2020), www.scientificamerican.com/article/corona virus-responses-highlight-how-humans-have-evolved-to-dismiss-facts-that-dont-fit-their-worldview/.

in the seventeenth century, has itself been displaced for many in the twenty-first century as non-scientific explanations are offered in its stead. This points to the possibility that the non-science explanation attached to COVID-19 is the equivalent of a religious explanation, so that the reliance on a nonscientific explanatory system that was at work in the fourteenth century, despite being somewhat obscure, is still visible in the dynamics of a more recent contemporaneous outbreak of a deadly pandemic.

Background to the Black Death

Karen Armstrong has offered this shorthand account of the European world at the time of the Black Death:

> During the fourteenth and fifteenth centuries, the Black Death had killed one third of the population of Christendom, and countries of Europe had been ravaged by such interminable strife as the Hundred Years War between England and France and the internecine Italian wars. Europeans had absorbed the shock of the Ottoman conquest of Christian Byzantium in 1453, and the papal scandals of the Avignon Captivity and the Great Schism. . .had caused many to lose faith in the institutional church. People felt obscurely afraid and found they could not be religious in the old way. (The new culture of Western Christendom) . . . would ultimately make the old mythological religion impossible, and it would seem that Western modernity was inherently hostile to faith.[17]

This summary overview of the fourteenth and fifteenth centuries points out that terrible afflictions – war and plague – were visited upon Christian Europe, and changes would come as a result. Some of those changes would affect the practice of faith and the trust faithful people had in the institution of the Church. Historically, this was a time of religious ferment in which many would lose confidence in the old ways and open themselves to such

[17] Karen Armstrong, *Battle for God* (New York: Alfred A Knopf 2000), 61.

change as would eventually be found in the drama of the Reformation. The Black Death contributed to these changes in the Christian Church and in the practices of faith, and this devastating pestilence, bubonic plague, brought unprecedented disasters to Christian people, which in turn led to widespread experiences of insecurity about life and livelihood. Violence arose from of that experience of insecurity. The insecurities grounded in fear led people to attempt to control uncontrollable events. Outbreaks of violence expressed bootless efforts to stem the lethal course of events associated with the bubonic plague, and that violence was directed by society's power holders, Christians, against those whose status in society was such that they could easily be blamed for the terrible afflictions.

Yersinia pestis

No textbook on disease and epidemiology would ever allow that *Yersinia pestis*, the bacterium responsible for the Black Death[18] – bubonic plague – was a punishment from God. Yet it was this understanding that commanded the views of the millions of Christians afflicted by the plague beginning in the mid-fourteenth century. Although 1348–51 were the peak years of the plague, the plague was not totally suppressed after this initial outbreak; and the Black Death would recur at various times over the remainder of the century, with outbreaks lasting up into the nineteenth century.

Originating in the Gobi desert and following the trade routes of Central Asia, the Black Death would reach Crimea in 1347. Carried along on caravans and the seafaring trade routes, the plague entered Europe through

---

[18] Some uncertainty surrounds the etiology of the Black Death. Some researchers have made the case that the plague originated in a hemorrhagic virus akin to Ebola. Brian Bossak, an environmental health scientist at Georgia Southern University "is among those who suspect a hemorrhagic virus – which causes bleeding and fever, like ebola – swept through 14th-century Europe. The high lethality, rapid transmission and periodic resurgences seen in the Black Death are characteristic of a virus." Wynne Parry, "Molecular Clues Hint at What Really Caused the Black Death," *Live Science* (September 7, 2011), www.livescience.com/15937-black-death-plague-debate.html.

the port of Genoa and then onto the Italian peninsula.[19] Spread by fleas that found hosts in the black rats found on merchant ships or caravans, the plague moved rapidly from Italy to the rest of Europe, then proceeded to enter and afflict North Africa and Western Asia as well. This natural disaster came on the heels of the Great Famine of the second decade of the fourteenth century, which, because of climate and weather changes, created massive food shortages, led to starvation and even cannibalism, and left a legacy of vulnerability to disease due to hunger and malnutrition. That legacy is also a part of the story of the Black Death.[20] The weakening of social, economic and, for present purposes, religious institutions is also a part of the legacy of the Black Death. So, for example, Karen Armstrong noted that the disasters of these two centuries led to a loss of faith in the institutional Church. One can only surmise the negative affect of the plague on those who had lived faithfully under the protection and nurture of the Church. The lives of everyday Christians were undoubtedly altered as the Church's defense against the plague, prayer, came to be regarded as less than effective as a means for addressing the challenges of mass starvation, inevitable suffering and the prospect of likely and sudden death. Among consequences of the Black Death were "new attitudes toward death, the value of life, and of one's self. It kindled a growth of class conflict, a loss of respect for the Church, and the emergence of a new pietism (personal spirituality) that profoundly altered European attitudes toward religion."[21]

The disease ravaged the countryside and entered towns, villages and cities. Infected fleas infected rats, and infected rats spread the disease to other rats. The hosts died but the fleas then attached to humans as they had the rats. Thus did the human population come to play the role of hosts with a staggering loss of life, generally accepted numbers being over 25 million

---

[19] John Kelly, *The Great Mortality: An Intimate History of the Black Death* (London: Harper Perrenial, 2005, 2013), 39.

[20] Ibid., 59–62.

[21] Lynn Nelson, "The Great Famine (1315–1317)/and the Black Death (1346–1351)," *Lectures in Medieval History*, www.vlib.us/medieval/lectures/black_death.html. Teofilo Ruiz has argued that the plague brought a new skepticism about Church authority.

dead representing anywhere from one third to two thirds of the population of Europe. The plague inspired fear and dread as it spread rapidly over large geographic regions. When it arrived in a population center, it would present one of three different forms: *bubonic plague*, which involved the lymph system from which developed enlarged and blackened pus-filled lymph glands – the "bubos" which appeared in the armpits and groin and provided visible evidence of the presence of "Black Death." Bubonic plague, which can still be found in various locales around the world today and is curable with tetracycline, was fatal in over half of those who contracted it. But the plague could also arrive as *pneumonic plague*, which attacked the respiratory system and was always fatal, or as a massive infection that entered the blood stream, *septicemic plague*, which was also fatal whenever it was contracted.[22] According to Lynn Nelson,

> The plague lasted in each area only about a year, but a third of a district's population would die during that period. People tried to protect themselves by carrying little bags filled with crushed herbs and flowers over their noses, but to little effect. Those individuals infected with bubonic would experience great swellings ("bubos" in the Latin of the times) of their lymph glands and take to their beds. Those with septicaemic would die quickly, before any obvious symptoms had appeared. Those with respiratory also died quickly, but not before developing evident symptoms: a sudden fever that turned the face a dark rose color, a sudden attack of sneezing, followed by coughing, coughing up blood, and death.[23]

Pneumonic plague could be spread from person to person. This highly contagious disease has been described as "explosive in the manner of nuclear chain reaction," with John Kelly quoting a Sicilian chronicler of the disease:

Kelly, *The Great Mortality*, 21–23.
Nelson, "The Great Famine (1315–1317)/and the Black Death (1346–1351)."

Breath spread the infection among those speaking together. . .and it seemed as if the victim[s] were struck all at once by the affliction and [were] shattered by it . . .. Victims violently coughed up blood, and after three days of incessant vomiting for which there was no remedy, they died, and with them died not only everyone who talked with them but also anyone who had acquired or touched or laid hands on their belongings.[24]

If pneumonic plague was 95–100 percent lethal, septicemic plague was even worse. What we know of this form of plague from twentieth century outbreaks surely applied to the fourteenth-century experience: "During one outbreak of septicemic plague in the early twentieth century, the average survival time from onset of symptoms to death was 14.5 hours."[25] This form of the pestilence was so virulent that those afflicted with it could begin the day feeling fine and with no anticipation be dead by afternoon.

European Christians at the time of the Black Death faced a one in three chance of contracting the disease, with death a likely outcome. Some survived bubonic plague, but as noted, pneumonic and septicemic plague were inescapably and inevitably fatal.

Without going into more detail about the horrors of the Black Death – and superb accounts of the Black Death are available[26] – it should not strain credulity to accept that European Christians experienced enormous fear, anxiety and insecurity given what they encountered with the Black Death. To know that the pestilence was on the move, that it had visited a near-by village or had entered one's hometown was to experience enormous apprehension and insecurity. Death was everywhere. The prospect of one's own demise was a constant worry. Bodies that could not be buried swiftly enough were part of the landscape as efforts to clear the streets and sick rooms were everywhere failing to keep pace with the production of corpses. Once the Black Death reached one's hometown, village or city, one could

[24] Kelly, 22. [25] Ibid.

[26] See Kelly; Philip Ziegler, *The Black Death* (New York: Harper Perennial, 2009)

expect to see a third of one's neighbors – and one third of one's family and those counted among one's loved ones – perish. Responses to the plague included more than fear and insecurity, however. Responses also included outbreaks of violence.

Anti-Semitism Unleashed

The reason for such suffering as had been inflicted with the plague was mysterious to the fourteenth century European Christian, but religion was the primary explanatory system available and thus the resource for understanding such a calamity. If the plague were a punishment from God, then penance was called for; if the plague somehow involved enemies of the faith bent on aggravating or extending the destruction of the Black Death, then the appropriate response was retaliation. Common folks as well as community and Church leaders speculated on the question of responsibility for the plague. If the plague had been sent by God, then the Church and its leaders were responsible for protecting the vulnerable. But the Church and its leaders seemed powerless. Stories abound from the period that tell of priests abandoning their responsibilities, fleeing communities where the dying or their families were calling for last rites. Priests were viewed as hypocrites seeking to save themselves, and the fact that they fled infected people and infected communities exposed their lack of faith and commitment to their priestly vows. These developments led to resentments and charges of worldliness and corruption against the clergy. And no answer seemed adequate to the question, "Why was it so indiscriminate?" The Black Death killed innocent children as well as adult sinners. If the Black Death were related to divine justice, theological problems arose, since the Christ event was believed to have restored relations between humanity and God once and for all. The idea that God had unloosed such vengeance did not fit well in that understanding. God had, after all, promised Noah after the flood not to destroy humanity again, and in the mid-fourteenth century people were living in the terrible fear that the Black Death heralded the end of the world.

The idea that the pestilence was the result of foul air – a sometimes-professed explanation – or the vengeful act of an angry God set on punishing an offending humanity were finally inadequate explanations. On the religious front, Christians were not used to viewing God as so brutal and uncaring as to justify so deadly a pestilence as the Black Death, and this generated in everyday Christians insecurities as to the power of the Church to provide protection against God's wrath. Yet there were nonreligious efforts to stem the spread of the pandemic. In an effort to slow the rapid spread of the disease from one region, city or town to another, communities imposed isolation tactics. Pedro IV of Aragon, for instance, attempted to isolate the plague in his kingdom by imposing a quarantine.[27] Medical historians look back at this period in the fourteenth century as the moment when public health efforts first got underway in Europe: "the concept of a single, centrally controlled board of public health was born of the Black Death."[28] Few human efforts, however, given the ignorance about the disease's etiology and the generally poor state of medical knowledge, could allay fear of the disease or comfort those living under threat of imminent death. So the search for an explanation and a way to understand what was happening turned to more traditional enemies. And in Christian Europe the most traditional of enemies were the Jews.

So why was there a response of violence to this natural disaster? Complex though an answer to this question must inevitably be, clearly violence was involved in the effort to understand the cause and the meaning of the pestilence. Violence represented direct action aimed at exerting control over the uncontrollable; and it was also a fear-driven response, a lashing out against otherwise uncontrollable forces threatening life and livelihood. The violence turned outward – there would also be an inward response – akin to that of the "bully" who uses intimidation, threats and violence to force submission of a victim to the bully's will, thereby establishing the victim of the bully as weaker, inferior, "other." In this time of profound insecurity, Christians came to play the role of "bullies" who projected their own insecurities on select victims. And since God was not intervening to put an end to the plague and God was not saving the people who were praying and performing penance to stop the pestilence and all the

[27] Robert S. Gottfried, *The Black Death: Natural and Human Disaster in Medieval Europe* (New York: The Free Press, 1983), 52

[28] Ibid., 122.

dying, the insecurities went into the very heart of faith. Vulnerable, afraid and insecure, Christians living at the time of the Black Death turned outward to identify the true enemy, the cause and agent of disaster, and they would seek to exert power against that enemy in hopes of controlling it. They would seek to fight it. So, they directed violence at identifiable and believed-to-be deserving targets, attributing responsibility for the destruction of medieval life to those deemed "other" – meaning non-Christians who possessed a long-standing history as enemies of the faith. In the wake of the experience of vulnerability and powerlessness accompanying the plague, these "others" – these victims of projected insecurities – also became scapegoats. And as such these victims – Jews – received the blame for all the death and destruction along with the judgment that if force was needed to stop the onslaught of disease, force would be used, even lethal force.

Given that Christians resorted to violence in response to the plague, which raises questions of ethics and social psychology – our interest here – what can be said is that acts of violence arose from the overwhelming sense of insecurity with which people were living. They projected those insecurities on an "other" who had held the position of enemy of Christianity since the beginning of the faith in the first century. Responsibility for the anti-Jewish violence is to be laid in part at the feet of the institutional Church, which proved to be ineffective in offering defense and protection of Jews if, as was widely believed, the plague was a consequence of divine wrath against Christians. Jews were a convenient target for blame, for the Church had long preserved a legacy of hatred against Jews and Jewish communities.

The clergy and the educated – the ruling classes – were aware that Jews were not responsible for the plague. That the anti-Semitic views held widely among the Christian populace led to actual instances of violence was due to the failure of Church and Christian community leadership efforts to put a stop to the attacks, but the ruling classes feared the popular will and also saw the plague as a situation that could promote economic self-interest, given the fact that the Christian ruling class was heavily indebted to Jewish money lenders. Barons, military leaders, merchants and both city and country people involved in the local economy owed Jewish lenders large sums of money – Christians were prevented by usury prohibitions from loaning money at interest, but no such prohibition attached to Jews. Christian demands for capital therefore opened the money-lending business exclusively to those who could deal with lending money at interest – Jews. Indebtedness to Jewish business interests along with the "Christ killer" tag that had never dissipated in Western culture fueled resentments that found an outlet when the pestilence arrived. The violence aimed finally at the cruel end of actually exterminating Jews, and, terrible as that was, it had the practical economic effect of providing debt relief for Christians. It is always to be remembered that Jewish involvement in the money-lending business had been created by Christian demand.[29] Historian Johannes Nohl has written that the Black Death outbreak of anti-Semitic violence was propelled by widespread Christian hatred of the Jews for longstanding religious reasons related to Jewish involvement in Christ's crucifixion, but material profit motives explain why more was not done to quash the violence toward Jews. One chronicler of the time wrote that the "poison which killed the Jews was their wealth."[30] For indebted Christians, the killing of Jews during the Black Death amounted to an immediate cancelation of debts. Jacob Twinger, a chronicler of the time, wrote: "If the Jews had been poor, and rulers of countries had not been in their debt, they would never have been burnt."[31]

But they were burned. And the word "exterminate" is appropriately used to describe actions directed against Jews. The many attacks on European Jews at the time of the Black Death have been well chronicled, and several are worth mentioning.

> Between the summer of 1348 and 1349, an unknown but large number of European Jews were exterminated. Some were marched into public bonfires, others burned at the stake, still others barbequed on grills or bludgeoned to

[29] Johannes Nohl. *The Black Death: A Chronicle of the Plague*. Trans. C. H. Clarke (New York: J. & J. Harper, 1924, 2006), 81, 190.

[30] Kelly, 253. [31] Nohl, *The Black Death*, 193–194.

death, stuffed into empty wine casks and rolled into the Rhine. In some localities, the killings were preceded by show trials; in other cases, there were no legal proceedings – sometimes not even an accusation. Jews were killed as prophylactic measure.[32]

Among justifications for the violence Christians used against Jews was the unfounded fear that Jews, taking orders from a secret Jewish community, conspired to murder Christian children and poison wells because it was widely accepted by Christians that the Jews were trying to exterminate them. Acts of violence among Christians then took on a kind of preemptive self-defense posture. Convinced that Jews were engaged in well-poisoning in various European locales, townspeople acted with deadly force. Christians killed the entire Jewish population in a town in Province, and the estimate is that 50,000 Jews were killed for the same reason in Burgundy.[33] The town council in Strasbourg tried to protect Jews in the community from the citizen uprising against the Jews, but the merchant's guild deposed the council and the newly installed replacement councilors, all anti-Semitic, saw to it that 2,; 000 Jews were burned to death.[34] Pogroms, actual organized massacres of Jews, got underway in Europe. Mass killings of Jews occurred in Esslingen, Eger and Nuremburg. In Basel, the Jews of the area were rounded up and imprisoned in a wooden shed on an island in the Rhine, the shed then being set on fire. Jews in Austria, Italy and Spain met similar fates, and torture was often used to gain confessions:

> Special 'Jewish tortures' were also available to interrogators. One technique was to place a crown of thorns on a prisoner's head, then smash it into the skull with a mailed fist or blunt instrument. Another was to place a rope of thorns between

---

[2] Kelly, 140.

[3] Nohl, 182. Town officials in Strasbourg defended the Jews from the poisoning accusations.

Gottfried, 74.

a prisoner's legs and then yank it up into the crotch and scrotum.[35]

These incidents of torture and slaughter were not rare and isolated but common throughout Europe and reported widely. One deadly irony of the entire well-poisoning attack was that the water supplies at this time in towns and villages were sources of typhus, dysentery and other water-borne diseases, and Jews had learned to avoid using the local wells. They apparently had acquired enough knowledge to associate water supply contamination with illness, and they warned their non-Jewish neighbors about the association of wells to sickness. That Jews avoided using wells, however, raised more suspicions against them – suspicion itself being a signal of insecurity – and as Nohl remarks "the people were incensed against the Jews, and they [i.e., the Jews] could expect no justice."[36]

The response to the insecurities created by fear of the Black Death led Christians to engage in murderous attacks on Jews. The programmatic effort to exterminate Jews amounted to genocide, and the attacks in different areas of Europe amounted to pograms. Of course not all Christians joined in the killing or supported it. There were Christian people who engaged in violence, but in the violence/nonviolence dialectic, there were also Christians opposed to acts of violence toward the Jews. The medical faculties of the universities of Paris and Montpellier objected to the attacks on Jews and stated that the accusations leveled against Jews were unfounded. Pope Clement VI, in a bold step, objected to the killings of Jews and tried to provide some guidance for his Church. He issued a bull condemning the murdering of Jews in Avignon, where the plague killed fifty percent of the population.[37] Wrote Clement "it cannot be true that the Jews … are the cause … of the plague … for [it] affects the Jews themselves."[38] The violence to which Christians resorted was not everywhere by everyone endorsed, and like the original Strasbourg councilors and the medical faculty who declared objections, Clement VI is recalled as a strong voice of reason who sought to stem a tide of violence he knew did not originate with Jews.

[35] Kelly, 140. [36] Nohl, 191. [37] Kelly, 161. [38] Ibid., 253.

The Flagellants – Violence Turned Inward

That insecurities can give rise to violence and be directed outwardly toward "others" is clearly illustrated by the Christian response to the Black Death. But during the Black Death violence was also directed inwardly. Not long after the outbreak of plague began a spiritual movement called "flagellism" attracted those seeking a different kind of spiritual response to the plague. Flagellism – self-flogging as atonement for sin – had been known in Europe since the eleventh century and may have come into use at the time of the millennium change when many Christians thought Christ's return was scheduled. The monks who first practiced it – who took it up as a spiritual practice, that is – did so to appease God's vengeance against sinners. The mortification of the flesh they practiced was meant to atone for personal sins. Flagellation did not become a collective movement until the mid-thirteenth century[39] when crop failures, wars and disease convinced many faithful that God was inflicting his wrath on humanity for sin and offense.

The Flagellants, as a collective, formed roving bands with men in front and women taking up the rear of traveling columns. They traversed the Italian and German countryside, even moving into England at one point although unsuccessfully, baring their backs and scourging themselves until the blood flowed. The Flagellants formed groups of up to 300 participants, and they wore white robes marked with red crosses front and back. Each group had a leader – a "father" – who heard confessions, imposed penance, and granted absolution. Observed Jean Froissart, a chronicler of the time:

> The penitents went about, coming first out of Germany. They were men who did public penance and scourged themselves with whips of hard knotted leather with little iron spikes. Some made themselves bleed very badly between the shoulder blades and some foolish women had cloths ready to catch the blood and smear it on their eyes, saying it was miraculous blood. While they were doing penance, they sang very mournful songs about nativity

Ibid., 265.

and the passion of Our Lord. The object of this penance was
to put a stop to the mortality, for in that time ... at least
a third of all the people in the world died.[40]

The Flagellants were seen as martyrs atoning for the sins of the world
and thereby acting to prevent any increase in suffering.[41] They performed
their masochistic acts in town centers, attracting not only attention but often
admiration from the townspeople who opened their homes to them and
provided them with food and candles for use in their rituals. Some town
councils in Germany even provided them with funds.[42] Robert Gottfried
attributes the attractiveness of the Flagellants to "the general dissatisfaction
with the clergy, who were seen as corrupt and incapable of assuaging the
pain of the Black Death in any way. By contrast, the Flagellants appeared
honest, novel and pure of heart. They claimed to be able to ward off the
devil, as well as plague."[43] Their blood and hair and nail clippings were
regarded as relics and "there are even records of some villagers bringing
corpses so that that flagellants could resurrect them."[44] Admired though
they were, by the end of 1348 the Flagellants seemed to have run their
course. Stories circulated about sexual improprieties and the movement
lurched toward millenarianism. They lost the support of respectable lay
authorities. By the fall of 1349, Pope Clement VI sought from the Sorbonne
faculty its opinion of the Flagellants, their conclusion being that they were
"supported by certain fatuous priests and monks, were enunciating doctrines and opinions which were beyond evil, erroneous and fallacious."[45]
Clement, who had originally tolerated the Flagellants and even joined them
in a procession, had soured on them after receiving such reports, and he
issued a bull forbidding the Flagellants from undertaking any public
penance:

Already the Flagellants, under pretense of piety have spilled
the blood of the Jews ... and frequently also the blood of
Christians. ... We therefore command our archbishops and

---

[40] Gottfried, 70. [41] Ibid., 71. [42] Ibid. [43] Ibid. [44] Ibid. [45] Ibid., 72.

> suffragans . . . as well as the laity, to stand aloof from the sect
> and never again to enter into relations with them"[46]

After Clement's bull, the movement fell apart. By 1350 it had all but disappeared.

Two matters regarding the Flagellants relevant to Christianity and violence are noteworthy. First, Christians who joined the Flagellants pursued penance and acts of atonement in the face of what they believed was an angry God, and they did so by resorting to violence. Their violence took the form of a brutalizing spiritual practice. Self-flagellation was long known as an accompaniment to penance and was an acknowledged spiritual practice in Christianity. Mortification of the flesh through self-scourging, a practice recalling the flagellation of Christ prior to his crucifixion, had been practiced by such luminaries as St. Francis and the Augustinian monk, Martin Luther. So violent acts involved in a human effort to appease a wrath-filled and offended deity were not always turned outward toward others but could take an inward direction. The Flagellants did, as a matter of course, however, turn their violence outward toward others, and it turned toward the "other" who had long been the object of Christian hatred and violence – the Jew. The Flagellants preached anti-Semitism.[47] They contributed to the violent cruelty directed at Jews by Christians during the height of the Black Death in the mid-fourteenth century.

Insecurity

The Black Death has served to illustrate the fact that violence can erupt when persons experience enormous insecurity. To be a European in the mid-fourteenth century was to be subject to the prospect of imminent death – painful and sudden death in some forms of plague – and such suffering as the plague caused proved bewildering. It was difficult to fit such an event into any coherent theology, for even if God punished sinners, this form of punishment seemed beyond all understanding. It was harsh and indiscriminate, and the Church, where God's faithful sought refuge and protection, offered no protection. Prayer was no weapon against plague or

Kelly, 268. [47] Ibid., 263.

a source even of solace. Church leaders, including local priests who fled their parishes often showed themselves to be less than committed to their priestly vows, and faithful people felt abandoned, cut off from saving sacraments and left to face death without understanding why. The suffering experienced at this time led many to conclude that there was no longer reason to show restraint in their moral lives, and many gave in to debauchery and a rampant Epicureanism. The pursuit of pleasure in the face of so deep and immediate an uncertainty about life and one's prospects for survival marked vulnerability in the face of the plague: this was a major theme in Bocaccio's *Decameron*, a major work of Italian literature whose many characters were all on a journey to flee plague-beset cities.

Many Christians at the time of plague expressed their fears and insecurities through violence. They scapegoated Jews, holding them responsible for well poisoning and the slaughter of Christian children; and they organized, sometimes though local governmental actions, to kill Jews. Even when they turned the violence inward, as the Flagellants did, they did not avoid the eventual outward turn of cruelty toward the Jewish others. Robert Gottfried has written that the Christian Church, which might have – and let us say should have – restrained the outward turn of violence toward Jews, failed the faithful by not providing "solace or support during the crisis" and it "failed to give spiritual comfort."[48] The Church could not restrain the violence Christians unleashed in Europe in the wake of the plague onslaught.

Insecurity and its relationship to violence is but one of four elements under consideration in this volume, and the example of the European Black Death is a dramatic – perhaps an overly dramatic – example of what can happen when even faithful Christians are subjected to the extraordinary pressures of so great a trauma as the Black Death conveyed to a whole civilization. Christianity, one could say, has within its teachings and practices restraints on the kind of violence that broke out during the Black Death, but the historical reality is that the Church did not succeed in directing that faithful persons – good Christians – observe these restraints. The anti-Jewishness that found new life and a new virulence during this

[48] Gottfried, 84.

period had long been a part of the Christian story, and it was never repudiated by Christians who continued to see Jews as enemies. What happened during this period previews what would happen centuries ahead when another form of virulent anti-Semitism would come out of Germany, prompted by the insecurities of a defeat in war and a total economic dislocation that gave rise to another pogrammatic effort directed again at a traditional enemy in Christian Europe, a scapegoat, that "someone to blame." Out of that historical chaos emerged an even more efficient form of genocide.

The role of insecurity is worth noting. It was mentioned earlier that the elements under consideration can in different analyses be at one time foregrounded and at other times backgrounded, and in this section we have intentionally foregrounded the element of insecurity to illustrate how it affected violence among Christians during the time of the Black Death. But for all the violence perpetrated by Christians, other Christians would criticize it and speak out against it. Academics and town councilors and even the Pope through an official pronouncement would condemn the violence. There is no predictable course of action that all Christians can be expected to take when, in dire circumstances of enormous fear and anxiety, they make efforts to conform action and faith. Christian people saw themselves as the victims of punishment from God. They took on the role of inflictors of punishment on those threatening social harmony and their community's identity as well as their individual lives. All four elements could be extracted in a more extended analysis, but here our chore has been to emphasize the fear and anxiety of those living in a time of overwhelming insecurity. The fact of insecurity, which is a way of speaking about the loss of trust in the explanatory systems that help one make sense out of one's world, can lead to violence. People unhitched from the pillars of meaning that guide them through life may out of fear scapegoat, stereotype and even kill to express that fear. Their frustrations and their inability to cope with insecurity when it reaches such profound depths can lead to terrible, even murderous, results: it did among Christians during the Black Death. Insecurity is always a potential source of violence, even among Christians for whom the restraints of faith did not prove powerful enough to overcome fear and open nonviolent pathways of action.

4 The Violence/Nonviolence Dialectic

Christian people are no strangers to violence, either as perpetrators or as victims. The "violence/nonviolence dialectic" element we focus on in this section points to the ways Christian people have opted to justify and engage in – or oppose – violence, doing so in ways that they believe conform their action to their Christian faith. There is significant diversity among Christians on this issue, but that diversity illustrates that there is no single viewpoint on the legitimation of violence and how in various circumstances it might be defended as consistent – or inconsistent – with the tenets of Christian faith.

The issue that most dramatically illustrates the violence/nonviolence dialectic element in thinking about Christianity and violence is war. Three options for thinking about appropriate involvement for Christians in actual warfare deserve attention: holy war, just war, and pacifism. These options are relevant to thinking about war-related notions like using force and justifying coercion, and Christians are familiar with these options. As individuals and even as communities Christian people have associated themselves with one or another of them – there are pacifist Churches, for example, and a natural law tradition in Roman Catholicism that has long supported a just war position, although there are also Catholic pacifists and Catholics who have supported holy war ideas. These three options for thinking about the use of force are not compatible with one another, so this element will show, as did the insecurity element previously, that Christians will find different ways to address issues where uses of force press themselves as live options. Those options become live depending on circumstances confronted, differences in interpretation of core values upheld in the tradition, and different emphases on what the faith requires.

Christian Holy War

The contemporary use of the term "holy war" has achieved global familiarity mainly because of association with particular conflicts in the Muslim community. Islam, which did not acknowledge the modern Western liberal distinction between secular and sacred, did not distinguish secular war from holy wars – neither did the ancient Hebrews – but today the designation of a use of force as "holy war" means in popular parlance a way of identifying – even translating – the term "'jihad" despite Islamic theologians and modern Western scholars refusing to accept this meaning. Jihad is traditionally a term for the meritorious spiritual struggle to shun evil and make oneself a better person – the jihad of the heart – and it is relevant to facing temptations and working toward making Allah – God – the center of one's existence. This spiritual meaning, however, has expanded to mean something beyond the "greater jihad" of spiritual struggle as advanced in Islamic theology.[49] More broadly the term has come in contemporary usage to refer to violent conflicts involving religious motivation; and invoking the term usually associates with terrorist groups and political extremists motivated at least in part by religious concerns. At issue is the desire to advance nationalistic or ethnic interest, and politics and religion are at the center of holy war–jihad notions, so religion has an important part to play but its role cannot be disconnected from politics, nationalism and economic realities. As one scholar has observed, "In the twentieth century there were no purely religious wars waged solely for the sake of religion."[50]

In recent decades, there has been a surge of terrorist activities undertaken for self-proclaimed religious motivations; and theological doctrines have often been used to identify sacred or "holy terror."[51] The term "jihad" now means in popular parlance an idea of "holy war" even if that is not its original meaning or preferred conceptual designation, and today it points to political and ethnic extremism connected to groups undertaking terrorist activities that appeal to religious motivations. Extremism, which assumes some straying off a norm, means for present purposes the proclivity to resort to violence.

---

[9] The "lesser jihad" or the jihad of the sword is, according to the words of the Prophet Mohammed, outward struggle, which would include such matters as going into battle and using force to accomplish military objectives.

[0] Volkhard Krech. "Sacrifice and Holy War," in Wilhelm Heitmeyer and John Hagan, eds., *International Handbook of Violence Research* (Dordrecht: Kluwer Academic Publishers), 1012.

Bruce Lincoln, *Holy Terrors: Thinking about Religion after September 11* (Chicago: University of Chicago Press, 2003).

Holy war is the product of absolutist thinking, which is a complex notion in itself but includes the idea that authorization for using violence and going to war issues from a revelation of the divine and thus infallible arbiter of moral meaning – God. All monotheistic religions have experience with holy war, as do Hinduism and Buddhism and many other religions as well. Besides the specifics of Islamic jihad, there is a generic sense of holy war, which refers to any use of force and violence justified by appeal to divine authority.[52]

Early Christians knew of holy war in this generic sense. War under this rubric was justified and sanctified to the extent it conformed to and enacted the divine will. The earliest instance of generic holy war in Christianity may harken back to the Book of Revelation (19.11–21), where Christ, the "rider [who] is called Faithful and True" (v. 11), wages war against "the kings of the earth and their armies" (v. 19). The armies of heaven defeat the false prophet, the anti-Christ, with those who followed him being "thrown alive into the fiery lake of burning sulfur" (v. 20). This depiction of the overthrow of Satan and his minions, because it is so totalistic, is perhaps the most destructive instance of violence – at least a vision of violence – in Western religions. It is certainly an image that flies in the face of Christianity's message of love and peace. In the end, beyond the end of history, all of the enemies of Christ and His Kingdom are destroyed – all unbelievers – and that includes a goodly number of sentient beings. This is holy war in which Christ is the Warrior, and it is an idea that harkens back to the early Jewish notions of war in which Yahweh (a "name" and text marker for the divine in the Hebrew scriptures) is identified as Israel's warrior and protector. Israel did not have a standing army at the time of say, the Exodus or the "attack on Jericho," for it was Yahweh who conquered the enemies of Israel. Human agents performed actions like holding up a rod as the Israelites crossed the Red Sea or blowing horns while marching around the wall of Jericho, but it is Yahweh who enters actual combat and defeats Israel's enemies. Yahweh is the fighter, the defender, the army, not the people of Israel. In St. John's

---

[52] Lloyd Steffen, *Holy War, Just War: Exploring the Moral Meaning of Religious Violence* (Lanham, MD: Rowman and Littlefield, 2007), 182.

Book of Revelation, the concluding book of the New Testament, it is Christ who plays this divine role of triumphalist warrior.

Holy war as a guide to action was clearly not accepted by the early Church, although at an early church council, the Council of Arles (314 CE), two years after Constantine's conversion, military service was legitimized for Christians. Killing an enemy in battle was considered a sin for which atonement was required, and conscientious objectors were targeted for excommunication.[53] The Latin Fathers of the Church, Augustine in particular, following Cicero, would go on to develop a just war position, but a holy war notion was at play in the Persian Wars under Emperor Haerakleios in the seventh century; in Charlemagne's campaigns that involved forcibly converting the defeated opponents to Christianity; and in Otto the Great's expansion to the east wherein he made forcible conversion of the Slavs a goal of his warfare against them.[54]

The most significant "holy war" event – or series of events – in Christian history pertain to the eight papal-sponsored Crusades to Palestine that cover the eleventh to thirteenth centuries (1095–1291). As a Christian holy war, a Crusade was "a war on behalf of the papal church which in turn saw itself as the representative of God. Participation in a war of this kind, whose instigator was ultimately God himself, was considered a positive, commendable and redeeming act."[55]

The Crusades issued from two main causes: first, the desire to preserve pilgrimage to Jerusalem for Christians undertaking an act of penance for sins, and secondly to address Turkish threats to the Eastern Byzantine Empire. On this second point, Muslims had been in conflict with the Eastern Empire, which was centered in Constantinople, Byzantium. When the Muslim Turks defeated Byzantine forces at Manzikert in 1071 and took over Asia Minor, the Byzantine Empire was threatened. The Byzantine Emperor, Alexis, asked Pope Urban II for assistance, and in 1095, Urban convened the Council of Claremont and issued the call for the

---

Krech, "Sacrifice and Holy War," 1010. [54] Ibid., 1011.

Krech, 1011. Quoting Rainer C. Schwinges, "Kreuzzug als Heiliger Krieg" in Peter Hermann, ed., *Glaubenskrieg in Vergangenheit und Gegenwart* (Gottingen: Vandenhoeck Ruprecht, 1996), 102.

First Crusade. Urban believed the Crusade would heal the rift between the eastern and western Churches, which had occurred as the Great Schism of 1054,[56] and, as Karen Armstrong estimates, in 1096 a total of ten armies with more than 160,000 soldiers accompanied by numerous pilgrims and church officials joined the First Crusade to Palestine.[57] Urging the knights of Europe to stop fighting one another and join in common cause against the Muslim enemies of God, Urban sought to inspire the pilgrims to military action, saying of the Turks, "They are an accursed race, a race utterly alienated from God, a generation, forsooth, which has neither directed its heart nor entrusted its spirit to God." Accordingly, as Armstrong avers, "Killing these godless monsters was a Holy act," and it was declared a Christian duty to "exterminate this vile race from our lands."[58] Whereas it had been forbidden for pilgrims to carry arms into the holy land prior to Urban's proclamation, it was now an expectation. Christendom had declared war on Islam.

And the Crusades were holy war. It was war different from other medieval wars; it would draw on the papal understanding of the state as being essentially theocratic; it would involve knights as warriors who blessed the enterprise; and core to the objectives of those who participated were the theologically relevant objectives of receiving penance and earning a release from sin.[59] Christians have often invoked God on behalf of objectives that harm others and that impose force or even conduct actual wars against others. The conquistadors who conquered American natives in the sixteenth century provide an apt example. Greed and racism would have sufficed as motivation for this appalling invasion by the European conquerors, "but in the European climate of the time, they needed a theological

---

[56] The process for healing this rift began in 1964 when Pope Paul IV and Orthodox Patriarch Athenagoras met in Jerusalem to discuss how they might restore full communion, but obstacles to that end remain, the Orthodox refusal to acknowledge papal primacy, which renders the Orthodox church schismatic, being one such obstacle.

[57] Karen Armstrong, *Holy War: The Crusades and Their Impact on Today's World* (New York: Anchor Books, 1988, 2001), 3.

[58] Ibid. [59] Krech, 1011.

argument"[60]; and that reliance on theological justification gave the flavor of holy war to the conquistadors' military enterprises. Holy wars are often undertaken in an effort to subjugate a foreign culture, and, as in the case of the Christian Crusades against the Muslim Turks, the enemy is viewed as a threat to the holy warriors' salvation. Religion throws gasoline on the fires of aggression and provides a surplus of justification for violence. That surplus provides symbolic meaning beyond mundane political and economic motivations, providing religious sanctification for motivating an escalation of violence – though religion is still only one factor among several others.

Holy wars are distinct from wars that might claim religious dynamics in some way. The European Thirty Years War, for example, often thought to be the result of religious fanaticism, involved participants who did not identify as Protestant or Christian so much as they did Bavarian, Swedish or Bohemian, so that one recent researcher has concluded that war was "not primarily a religious war" at all but one that went on because unpaid armies could not be supplied or disbanded and stayed in the field for inordinately lengthy periods of time "nourished on plunder."[61]

The Crusades remain the archetypical Christian holy war, and – like all wars – it failed to accomplish all it intended. It did not achieve Urban's hope for Church unification. Divisions between east and west persisted, and although Christianity did identify a new common enemy – the Muslims, a "vile race" – Islam was not defeated. Christians, however, did succeed in identifying another Semitic group of non-Christian monotheists who, like the Jews, were believed to be enemies of God and whom they believed God wanted defeated through violence and bloodshed. The Crusades established a narrative for Christians that violence could be used to quash the enemies of the faith, a basic tenet of holy war.

In the violence/nonviolence dialectic, pacifism is the nonviolent counterpoint to holy war, and we shall discuss that separately, but it should be noted that Christians did offer resistance and opposition to

C. A. J. Coady "Violence and Religion," *Revue Internationale de Philosophie*, Vol. 67, no. 265(3) (2013): 253.
Ibid., 252.

holy war as Christian holy war. Missionary activity, although often involved in colonial suppression of native persons and the assertion of Eurocentric supremacy, can be nonviolent, and no instruction from the Gospels or other New Testament text urging Christians to take the Christian message into the world advocated or justified violence even if conversion was the aim. A model might be found in St. Francis of Assisi who, in his missionary work, pursued a kind of nonviolent holy war. St. Francis visited the caliph of Egypt during the Crusades; and at a time when Muslims and Crusaders were fighting near the Caliph's position, Francis met with the caliph with the intention of converting him and other Muslims to Christianity. He came in peace and conducted himself peacefully, perhaps even expecting martyrdom for his efforts, although the caliph probably respected Francis as a holy man and offered him no threat of harm. But the Crusades were not far from Francis' approach to missionary work. He had put a chalk cross on his back when he began his religious life in earnest upon leaving Assisi, and by that act he became a "cross bearer" or "Crusader."[62] Francis aimed his nonviolent crusade at converting the Muslims by show of example and through preaching and good works. Other missionary opponents of violence include Bishop Batoloemo de Las Casas and the Dominican theologian Anonio Montesinos who preached publicly against the Spanish genocide of the conquistadores, denouncing

> the cruelty and tyranny that you practice on these innocent people. Tell me by what right or justice do you hold these Indians in such cruel and horrible slavery. By what right do you do you wage such detestable wars on these people who live mildly and peaceably on their own lands . . . where you have consumed infinite numbers of them with unheard of murders and desolations.[63]

[62] *ZENIT Daily Dispatch*, "St. Francis and Christian-Muslim Relations, Interview with Lawrence Cunningham" March 29, 2006, www.ewtn.com/catholicism/library/st-francis-and-christianmuslim-relations-1631.

[63] Coady, 253.

Christians, like all religious people, make decisions about how they will be religious, and Christians can be found on both sides of the violence/ nonviolence dialectic element, even on the issue of holy war.

Just War

Since the fourth century, Christian moral theology has articulated an approach to war and uses of force that is, on the one hand, sympathetic to "realism" yet, on the other, holds open the possibility that such uses of force can be justified in accordance with Christian principles, teachings and ideals. This is known as the "just war" tradition and it represents a development consistent with natural law moral theology and natural law ethics. The natural law tradition predates Christianity, so in its origins it is not explicitly Christian even though it is the major philosophical approach to Roman Catholic moral theology today.

Natural law ethics holds to the idea that the natural endowment of reason suffices to discern what is good and right. Natural law Christians go one step further and attribute that natural endowment of reason in human beings to God and God's creative action. There are some indications Aristotle had a notion of just war, but the idea received attention and was developed more explicitly by Cicero, then further developed by St. Augustine, who then handed it over to the Christian moral tradition where Aquinas developed it further. Modifications and clarifications have continued to this day. Just war thinking still influences the ethics of war. It is appealed to in UN resolutions – the just cause of self-defense is explicitly acknowledged in article 51 of the UN Charter – and it can be found governing international law about warfare, humanitarian interventions and uses of force; and it provides philosophical support for international agreements concerning the rules of war. Just war thinking continues to play a large role wherever war or uses of force are contemplated because of some disorder, aggressive destructiveness or evil that reasonable persons of good will believe should be resisted, corrected and stopped. Many Christians find just war a natural law form of realism compatible with Christian values and justice concerns in a fallen, sinful world: it sanctions resistance to aggression, wrongdoing and evil.

Just war as it is understood today advances several criteria that structure the morally relevant issues that must then be considered in light of particulars. The criteria are nonspecific guidelines or *jus ad bellum* criteria, which determine whether an anticipated use of force is, indeed, morally justifiable, whether or not a use of force is actually employed. The criteria are as follows:

- legitimate authority,
- just cause,
- right intention,
- last resort,
- an outcome in which the good achieved outweigh the pain and destruction of war,
- the preservation of values that could not otherwise reasonably be preserved,
- and a reasonable hope of success.

Two other just war criteria, the *jus in bello*, govern conduct in the war: noncombatant immunity and proportionality of means.

The *jus in bello* criteria, first, protects noncombatants from harm and direct attack, and, second, prohibits evil means of waging war, even disallowing certain weapons and modes of warfare conduct if the weapon produces an effect disproportionate to the end of securing peace (e.g., chemical, biological and nuclear weapons).

Taken together these nine criteria identify justice concerns relevant to using force and coercion – or going to war. They identify no empirical specifics of any specific conflict situation. They frame moral deliberation around morally relevant concerns germane to the application of force. All nine must be satisfied when applied to a particular situation, and if the criteria, once applied, are satisfied, force, coercion – war itself – may be deemed permissible. The appeal of the theory is to reasoned and reasonable ethical guidelines that identify concerns of justice. Those guidelines then establish the ethical issues that must be addressed and resolved in any particular conflict situation; and they direct debate and moral deliberation over ethical issues as the facts of particular conflicts are established and then evaluated in light of the just war criteria.

St. Augustine's appeal to just war criteria – a shortened version from the modern articulation just presented – was based on the idea that war was a terrible evil that expressed human selfishness and a disorder that arose from "violence, revengeful cruelty, fierce and implacable enmity, wild resistance and the lust of power and such like."[64] Although today just cause for a just war locates least controversially in self-defense against aggression, Augustine located just cause for war in a punitive action: "It is generally to punish these things [the disorders just mentioned], when force is required to inflict punishment, that, in obedience, to God or some lawful authority, good men undertake wars."[65] Wars are waged to the end of bringing about peace and good order and they are the result not of choice but of necessity; and his truncated theory contains three criteria still part of contemporary just war thinking: legitimate authority, just cause and right intention.

The classic form of just war thinking is associated with Saint Thomas Aquinas (1225–74) who held that "just cause" for war is concerned to right wrongs, to restore what has been wrongfully seized, and to punish a state that fails to punish crimes committed by its own citizenry. Wrote Thomas in "Of War:"

> In order for a war to be just, three things are necessary. First, the authority of the sovereign by whose command the war is to be waged. For it is not the business of a private individual to declare war. ... Secondly, a just cause is required, namely, that those who are attacked should be attacked because they deserve it on account of some fault. [Quoting Augustine] "A just war is wont to be described as one that avenges wrongs, when a nation or state has to be punished, or to restore what it has seized unjustly." Thirdly, it is necessary that the belligerents

Augustine, *St. Contra Fauastum Manichaeum*. In John Langan, "The Elements of St. Augustine's Just War Theory," *The Journal of Religious Ethics*, Vol. 12, no. 1 (Spring 1984): 21.
Ibid., 22.

have a rightful intention, so that they intend the advance-
ment of good, or the avoidance of evil.[66]

In addressing the question whether it is permissible to kill in self-
defense, Aquinas offered another significant contribution to just war –
and beyond. He introduced the concept of "double effect." "Nothing
hinders one act from having two effects, only one of which is intended
while the other is beside the intention. ... Accordingly the act of self-
defense may have two effects: one, the saving of one's life; the other, the
slaying of the aggressor."[67] So victims of unjust aggression could repel
attackers even if lethal force were to be used, for doing so would satisfy the
demands of justice and the just cause criterion. But killing the attacker must
not be the intended aim – the intended aim is to repel and stop the attack
but, Thomas says, "It is not lawful for a man to intend the killing of a man in
self-defense"[68] and the use of force must be proportionate to the end of
restoring peace. If killing the attacker does occur as an unintended and
secondary consequence of the engagement with the attacker, the doctrine of
double effect could be applied to establish that the killing – unwanted
though it be – was permissible. The main intention – self-defense as just
cause – is morally justifiable, and the negative double effect – the killing –
occurred as a foreseen but unintended consequence. The doctrine of double
effect is alive and well today. It is, for instance, vital in contemporary
bioethics when end-of-life situations arise and pain management – a good
end – requires doses of medications that address pain but suppress breathing; and that suppression of breathing may – and usually does – lead to
a foreseen but unintended consequence, namely, the death of the patient.
Thus, through double effect, is active direct euthanasia avoided.

[66] Thomas Aquinas, "On War," *Summa Theologica, II, II Q. 40*, trans. Fathers of
the English Dominican Province. (Chicago: Encyclopedia Britannica, 1952), 578
[67] Thomas Aquinas, "Whether It Is Permissible to Kill a Man in Self-Defense?"
Summa Theologica, II-II, Q. 64 article 7, reprinted in *The Ethics of War: Classic
and Contemporary Readings*, eds. Gregory Reichberg, Henrik Syse and Endre
Begby (Malden, MA: Blackwell, 2006), 190–191.
[68] Aquinas, "On War," 911.

The Spanish Scholastics Francisco de Vitoria, Gabriel Vazquez, Francisco Suarez and Luis Molina Vitoria modified and extended just war thinking. Suarez, the most systematic and comprehensive of these authors, explored the *jus in bello* idea of noncombatant immunities and issues like deceiving the enemy.[69] Hugo Grotius, a Protestant Dutch theologian – often regarded as the father of international law – defended the idea that self-defense against injury was a natural right, one so secure even God could not subvert or challenge it.[70] The Reformation weakened any prospect of developing a Christian commonwealth in Europe, but both Catholic and Protestant theologians defended and employed just war thinking as it assumed the task of providing a means for thinking about how to limit the destructiveness of war. That just war might contribute to limiting violence was important in light of the religious wars of the sixteenth century, and limiting destructiveness of war is often cited as a reasoned justification for just war thinking even today. As Roman Catholic theologian Richard McBrien has written, "The purpose of just war theory . . . was not to rationalize violence but to limit is scope and method."[71]

That just war thinking serves to rationalize violence is a criticism often leveled at just war. The criticism is that war is a terrible evil and often military actions require moral justification in order to gain public support. Invoking just war provides that justification but doing so is simply wrongheaded. Pursuing conflict resolution through uses of force justified under just war rubrics ignores how often uses of force cannot be subject to rational control and inevitably fail to serve the purpose of serving justice and

---

[69] Christopher Shields and Daniel Schwartz, "Francisco Suárez," in Edward N. Zalta, ed., *The Stanford Encyclopedia of Philosophy* (Winter 2019 Edition), https://plato.stanford.edu/archives/win2019/entries/suarez/.

[70] Hugo Grotius, "The Theory of Just War Systematized (On the Law of War and Peace)," reprinted in *The Ethics of War: Classic and Contemporary Readings*, eds. Gregory Reichberg, Henrick Syse and Endre Begby (Malden, MA: Blackwell, 2006): 385–437.

Richard McBrien, *Catholicism: A Study Edition* (Minneapolis: Winston Press, 1981), 1036.

restoring peace. War – uses of coercive power and force – more often than not adds to injustice rather than mitigates or corrects it.

Yet just war thinking has not only a pedigree but a current life and even a sustainable future in Christian thought and practice. What just war offers, on the positive side, is a structure of moral concern that invites reasonable people of good will into conversation around justice concerns and empirical particulars, providing a way to frame moral deliberation in pursuit of peace and justice.

Adopted in secular frameworks like international law, just war also reflects concerns Christian just war theorists would say are consistent with addressing actual evils in the world. Those evils must be resisted and corrected while requiring that uses of force satisfy concerns of justice, which Christians are in the main committed to doing. As presented here, just war rests on a platform of value consistent with practical pacifism – force ought ordinarily not be used to settle conflicts. Just war is non-absolutist and realist to the extent that it can move through deliberation to a justification of a use of force in a particular circumstance as an exception to that underlying moral agreement that ordinarily force ought not to be used to settle conflicts. Just war is today the dominant perspective used by Christians to address injustices, resist evil and restore peace when it is necessary to deliberate under what circumstances violence might be applied to resist evil and injustice.

Pacifism

The case is often made – and the perception is widely held – that Christianity is a pacifist religion. The reasons for this go back to the Gospel presentations of Jesus' teaching, including the best known of those, the Sermon on the Mount. At Matthew 5.38 ff.[72], Jesus speaks as follows:

> You have heard that it was said, "An eye for an eye and a tooth for a tooth." But I say to you, Do not resist an evil

[72] See also the Gospel of Luke's version of this teaching, the Sermon on the Plain, at Luke 6.27, 28: "But I say to you that listen, Love your enemies, do good to those who hate you, bless those who curse you, pray for those who abuse you."

doer. But if anyone strikes you on the right check, turn the other one also; ... You have heard that it was said, "you shall love your neighbor and hate your enemy." But I say to you, Love your enemies and pray for those who persecute you, so that you may be children of your Father in heaven. (NRSV)

In this teaching, Jesus counsels – commands actually – forgiveness and repudiates vengeance and retribution. He goes so far as to say that one ought not to resist an evildoer, a radical position when it comes to thinking about Christianity and violence. Yet the idea of "not resisting an evildoer" does not have a large following in Christianity, even in the peace churches that arose at the time of the radical Reformation. The Mennonite Church, for instance, a well-known "pacifist church," acknowledges in a footnote to Article 22 governing "Peace, Justice and Nonresistance," that "In continuity with previous Mennonite confessions of faith, we affirm that non-participation in warfare involves conscientious objection to military service and a *nonresistant* [emphasis added] response to violence." Yet in the text of the article – not a footnote – are found these words: "The same Spirit that empowered Jesus also empowers us to love enemies, to forgive rather than to seek revenge, to practice right relationships, to rely on the community of faith to settle disputes, and *to resist evil* [emphasis added] without violence."[73] While acknowledging historical connection to a nonresistance-to-evil stance, the contemporary Mennonite declaration of principles on the issue of peace and justice stands in *resistance to evil* without violence rather than reaffirming without qualification *nonresistance to evil*. The two notions, both associated with pacifism and with Christian pacifism in particular, are not equivalent and clearly do not mean the same thing.

The meaning of nonresistance to evil as distinct from nonviolent resistance – these terms related to Christian pacifism in the dialectic of violence and nonviolence – deserves attention. Keeping in mind that "pacifism" writ

---

Mennonite Church USA, "Article 22. Peace, Justice, and Nonresistance." www .mennoniteusa.org/who-are-mennonites/what-we-believe/confession-of-faith /peace-justice-and-nonresistance/.

large represents a counterpoint to holy war and even to the realism of just war in that dialectic, both notions have been advanced by a pacifist Christian church – the Mennonites – but examination of the terms will reveal that nonviolence resistance is more in line with just war than with a nonresistance to evil notion. The difference between these two forms of pacifism can be discerned from a quick examination of a literal nonresister, Leo Tolstoy, and nonviolent resister, Rev. Dr. Martin Luther King, and to that task we now turn.

Nonresistance to Evil – Leo Tolstoy

A profound spiritual crisis, chronicled in his spiritual autobiography, *My Confession*, led Leo Tolstoy to a Christian faith that claimed at its heart an affirmation of Christ's teachings as recorded in the Gospels. This included the Sermon on the Mount and the specific teaching, "resist not evil," which was central to Tolstoy's ethic. Tolstoy held that two laws governed human existence, the law of violence and the law of love, and the law of love was Christianity in its purest form – nonresistance – while the law of violence involved persons in the structures and institutions that relied upon government and its authority to use violence to order society. "The true meaning of Christ's teaching consists in the recognition of love as the *supreme law* and therefore not admitting of exceptions," Tolstoy wrote, adding "the Christian teaching in its true meaning, recognizing the law of love as supreme, and permitting no exceptions in its application to life, ruled out any form of violence and consequently could not but condemn the whole structure of the world founded on violence."[74]

It is in the idea of "no exceptions" that we can locate Tolstoy's absolutism. He held that Christ's teachings were absolutely binding and no compromise must be made with them. He is an absolute pacifist whose vision was not directed to the end of social reform. He sought, rather, to repudiate the law of violence and the social, political and economic world

---

[74] Leo Tolstoy, "The Law of Love and the Law of Violence," in *A Confession and Other Religious Writings*, trans. Jane Kentish (Harmondsworth, UK: Penguin Books, 1987): 174–175.

built upon it, offering as an alternative a world conforming it in all respects to the law of love:

> If now in a moment of forgetfulness I may be so far carried
> away as to use violence for the defense of myself or others or
> my own property or that of others, I can no longer calmly
> and consciously serve that temptation, which destroys
> myself and other men. I cannot acquire property; I cannot
> use violence of any sort against any manner of man, with the
> exception of a child, and then only to save him from some
> evil that hangs over him; I cannot take part in any activity of
> the authorities having as its aim the defense of men and their
> property by violence; I can neither be a judge nor one
> sharing in court duties; I cannot be an executive or one
> sharing an executive position; I cannot contribute to others
> having others take part in courts and executive positions.[75]

Absolutists will inevitably contradict themselves, since, as a matter of logic, absolutes entail everything, including their own contradiction, and Tolstoy's Christian pacifism wound up contradicting itself and presenting not peace but destructiveness. A despiser of money and opposed to using government-sponsored transportation systems and even mail services, Tolstoy was afflicted with terrible pangs of conscience when a drought hit Russia and he was asked to use his international celebrity to raise funds to bring relief to thousands who were suffering hunger. He admitted to feeling "ashamed of himself" for having relented and for agreeing to do so. He was, in his own eyes, lending aid to the structures sustained by the law of violence even as they served the good end – the charitable and compassionate end one would think consistent with the teachings of Jesus – of helping to organize philanthropic efforts to ease suffering, feed the hungry and save lives.[76] Tolstoy's absolutism aimed at living in accord with the law of love, but it actually increased human suffering and would have contributed to

Quoted in George Rapall Noyes, *Tolstoy* (New York: Dover, 1968): 239.
Noyes, 248.

inflicting the violence of refusing aid had he not relented and agreed to help
feed the hungry.[77]

Tolstoy's absolutism encompasses a Christian pacifism based on a literal
reading of the Sermon on the Mount and the idea of "resist not evil." Most
persons who refer to Christian pacifism do not believe they are endorsing so
severe a pacifism as that which Tolstoy held – even Gandhi was not so
absolutist, refusing to criticize British resistance to Hitler and upholding the
right of a woman facing a rapist's attack to resist her attacker.[78]
Nonresistance, however, does represent a form of pacifism – a radical and
absolutist form of nonviolence – sustained by Christian teachings and
Christian values.

Nonviolent Resistance – Rev. Dr. Martin Luther King, Jr.

Pacifism upholds the centrality of nonviolence, and although advocates of
Christian nonviolence are often assumed to be absolutist pacifists like
Tolstoy, they are not. The Rev. Martin Luther King, Jr. was one of the
twentieth century's most ardent defenders of nonviolence, but his pacifism – if we can call it that – never took the form of nonresistance to evil.
Even when civil rights marchers were beaten and abused and refused to
fight back when attacked, they understood what they were doing as active
resistance to evil. Nonviolence was the means by which they would
"fight" against the evil. If nonresistance represents an extreme form of
pacifism, nonviolent resistance, as embodied by King (and Gandhi as
well), were stances that opposed oppression, resisted evil and aimed at

[77] For a discussion of Tolstoy's "demonic pacifism," see Steffen, *Holy War, Just
War*, 151–158.

[78] Mohandas Gandhi: "Gandhi further goes on to say that in the event of an assault,
however, the woman must use all her physical might to resist assault. 'When
a woman is assaulted, she may not stoop to think in terms of himsa or ahimsa. Her
primary duty is self-protection. She is at liberty to employ every method or
means that come to her mind in order to defend her honour. God has given her
nails and teeth. She must use them with all her strength and, if need be, die in the
effort. The man or woman who has shed all fear of death will be able not only to
protect himself or herself but others also through laying down his (or her) life'"
(H, 1-3-1942, p. 60). Quoted in Noyes, *Tolstoy*, 239.

converting oppressors through guilt over injustice and moving them toward justice.

Unlike the nonresistance of Tolstoy, nonviolent resistance did not dismiss government and laws and offer an alternative based on a rejection of the law of violence while embracing exclusively – absolutely – the law of love; rather, as the example of King and the American civil rights movement made abundantly clear, nonviolent resistance engaged with political authority. It sought to reform society through political and social action bent toward justice; and it was adamant in opposing laws and policies that were deemed oppressive, dehumanizing and unjust. Nonviolent resistance did not seek to destroy the political or social order; it sought to reform it. It sought to conform it to the demands of justice. That the Christian minister Martin Luther King, Jr. was thus engaged allows that this kind of nonviolent action for social change was consistent with Christian values and represented Christian action aimed at achieving justice. Nonviolent resistance is a position that stands squarely on the nonviolence side of the violence/nonviolence dialectic. The irony is that characterizing nonviolent resistance as a form of pacifism can be misleading, since nonviolent resistance has more in common with just war thinking than it does with the absolutist pacifism of a Leo Tolstoy.

The claim just made may seem odd and at least controversial if in fact not at all true. But the claim deserves consideration as an ethic King would have followed. King certainly affirmed nonviolence as central to his ethic and his politics, and nonviolence is the core value – the conceptual platform – of just war if we accept that as an ethic. The criteria of just war thinking provide a means to test whether an exception can be made to the common moral agreement underwriting just war as an ethic, namely, that ordinarily force ought not to be used to settle conflicts. That common agreement is not absolute, but it is principled and must hold in place until such time as the criteria of just war allow for an exception to it. The other move that would position nonviolent resistance to "fit" into a just war framework is to acknowledge that nonviolent resistance represents an application of force. (Gandhi's *satyagraha*, which, along with Jesus sermon on the Mount ethic, provided King with inspiration, is even defined as "soul force" and Gandhi used martial images to explain it to readers.)

Nonviolent resistance is an application of force to achieve ends that could not be achieved through negotiation, mediation and arbitration. With nonviolence a core value to his Christian ethic of engagement with adversaries, King avowed an ethic of resistance to evil with nonviolence then to be employed as an actual use of force designed to achieve moral and political ends. Note the just war criteria in italics in the following.

King appealed to religious sources and conscience to establish *legitimate authority* for using nonviolence as a mode of resistance to evil in conflict situations. Nonviolence as a form of resistance is a use of force, even coercion – Gandhi was even clearer and more articulate on this point[79] – but clearly the act of resistance was aimed at addressing injustice, changing the hearts of the oppressor, and bringing about the goal of justice and peace. King observed a common moral agreement that force, even the force of nonviolent resistance, should not be used if it can be avoided (*last resort*), and he held that this moral agreement governed action prior to any potential use of nonviolent resistance in a conflict situation. King always advocated alternatives to nonviolent resistance, engagements with adversaries that would first rely upon negotiation, arbitration or mediation. If the injustice faced required employing the force of nonviolent resistance, King grounded authority for its use in transcendent sources, and access to this source was through conscience and its demand of Christian duty (*legitimate authority*):

> Your highest loyalty is to God, and not to the mores or folkways, the state or the nation of any man-made institution. If any earthly institution or custom conflicts with God's will, it is your Christian duty to oppose it. You must never allow the transitory, evanescent demands of man-made institutions to take precedence over the eternal demands of almighty God.[80]

[79] Lloyd Steffen "Gandhi's Nonviolent Resistance: A Justified Use of Force?" *Journal of Philosophy and the Contemporary World*," Vol. 15, no. 1 (June 2008): 68–80.

[80] Quoted in Hanes Walton Jr., "King's Philosophy of Nonviolence," in Thomas Siebold, ed., *Martin Luther King Jr.* (San Diego: Greenhaven Press, 2000), 88.

For King, the *just cause* for nonviolent resistance was to be found in the conditions of injustice and oppression. Nonviolence sought to address the injustice by fighting racism, advancing integration, opposing economic and political inequality, and resisting violence, and he once remarked, ironically, that "the most pervasive mistake I made was in believing that white Christian clergy" would lend support to his efforts "because our cause was just."[81] Additionally, as mentioned, King's advocacy of nonviolent resistance expressed a Christian vision of working for justice to the end of achieving peace, so that the means of action – nonviolence – embody the values associated with the end of peace: the means justify the ends (*preservation of values*). And King believed that his efforts had a *reasonable hope of success* if one looked beyond short term obstacles toward the longer arc of history: "The method of nonviolence is based on the conviction that the universe is on the side of justice. . . . [The nonviolent resister] knows that in his struggle he has cosmic companionship."[82] It is also worth noting that King believed that some nonviolent tactics like bus boycotts or work stoppages could wind up harming innocent persons – the children, say, of the boycotters – so this reinforced the "last resort idea" while also demonstrating awareness that the means of opposition must seek to avoid harming innocents (*noncombatant immunity*), which King did in his strategizing for resistance efforts. In the end he was convinced his "method" of nonviolence was most conducive to bringing about the end of peace while also observing the *criterion of proportionality*.

King, of course, did not present nonviolent resistance as a form of just war thinking. The fact remains, however, that as much as it is

[81] Martin Luther King, Jr., "Playboy Interview," in *Testament of Hope: The Essential Writings and Speeches* (Harper and Row, 2003): 344.

[82] King, "A Nonviolence and Racial Justice," in *Testament of Hope*, 8, 9. King would be even more explicit about victory and the nature of the victory: "Be assured that we'll wear you down by our capacity to suffer, and one day we will win our freedom We will not only win freedom for ourselves; we will so appeal to your heart and conscience that we will win you in the process, and our victory will be a double victory" *(reasonable hope of success)*. Ibid: 257.

presented as a form of Christian pacifism, it is a peculiar form of
pacifism to say the least and it can be shown, as demonstrated here, to
"fit" a just war picture where the aim of the effort is not nonresistance
but nonviolent resistance. It is an application of force to achieve the
ends of justice and it is grounded in the idea that ordinarily one ought
not use force – even nonviolent force – to settle conflicts, but only
when the evil faced requires active resistance and other nonviolent
means – negotiation, arbitration and mediation – are not working.
Nonviolent resistance is a non-absolutist form of pacifism; and just
war is a non-absolutist structure for deliberating the possibility of
justified uses of force, which includes the force at issue in nonviolent
resistance.

Reinhold Niebuhr on Pacifism

Nonviolent resistance is a mode of addressing evil that many Christians
will say satisfies the need to address injustice actively and in accord with
Christian values and the Christian message of peace. This view has
detractors, perhaps none so well-known as Reinhold Niebuhr, the most
prominent American Protestant theologian of the twentieth century,
who wrote an article, "Why the Christian Church Is Not Pacifist."
Niebuhr argues that pacifists, which seems to include for him both
nonresisters and nonviolent resisters, do not have standing to accuse
the Christian Church of apostasy in advocating pacifism because the
Christian Gospel "refuses to equate the Gospel with the 'law of love.'"
Rather, Niebuhr goes on to argue,

> Christianity is a religion which measures the total dimen-
> sion of human existence not only in terms of the final
> norm of human conduct, which is expressed in the law of
> love, but also in terms of the fact of sin. It recognizes that
> the same man who can become his true self only by
> striving infinitely for self-realization beyond himself is
> also inevitably involved in the sin of infinitely making his
> partial and narrow self the true end of existence. It
> believes, in other words, that though Christ is the true

norm ("the second Adam") for every man, every man is
also in some sense a crucifier of Christ.[83]

Niebuhr, a "realist," accuses pacifists of naiveté for not taking into account
the harsh reality of human sin, which subverts the pacifist ideal with an
unrealistic view of human nature. The tragedy of human sin, Niebuhr
argues, renders any pacifistic theology "heretical"[84] – that is his word –
and to keep the reality of human sin front and center he offers a defense of
just war, unaware that underwriting just war *as an ethic* is a common moral
agreement Christians should be expected to avow, namely, that ordinarily
force ought not be used to settle conflicts. It is this underlying principle to
which reasonable people of good will assent that renders just war itself
a kind of practical pacifism. For the reality is that the criteria of just war are
difficult to satisfy, they all must be satisfied, and to satisfy the criteria at the
opening of a conflict that seems justified under just war criteria does not
mean that those criteria do not continue to monitor the use of force.
Justification for uses of force can be withdrawn if the criteria are violated,
and this happens more often than not: finding an actual war that was a just
war under just war criteria from beginning to end, is a difficult chore. To
use force in ways that violate the criteria can render a seemingly just war an
unjust war despite original claims that the use of force was, in fact, morally
justified.

Concluding Remarks on Christians and War

In considering Christianity and violence, attention must be given as done
here to the topic of war. Christians have a long history of engaging in power
politics and they have been involved as Christians in warfare over the
centuries. Protestants and Catholics in the post-medieval period were
engaged in numerous conflicts. In the sixteenth century, for example, the
Royal Catholic League fought against Protestant Huguenots (1652–98),

---

Reinhold Niebuhr, "Why the Christian Church Is Not Pacifist," in
Mark Juergensmeyer and Margo Kitts, eds. and intro., *Princeton Readings in
Religion and Violence* (Princeton: Princeton University Press, 2011), 46.
Ibid., 53.

and medieval serfdom was the cause of the Great Peasant War in Germany
(1524–5). In the Peasant War, Martin Luther failed as a mediator between
serfs and landlords, finally encouraging the landlords to "stab, strike,
strangle these mad dogs,"[85] namely, the peasant serfs. And Luther also
became a savage critic of Jews when he discovered, to his surprise, that Jews
would not convert to his version of true Christianity. His 1543 work *On the
Jews and Their Lies* described Jews as a "base, whoring people, that is, no
people of God," whose property should be confiscated and who should be
forced into labor and denied any legal protections; he even goes so far as to
say that Christians "are at fault for not slaying them."[86] Luther advocated
the violent repression of the serfs' revolt and he conducted war against the
Jews without ever himself taking up arms against them.

In the seventeenth century, Sweden and Poland were mired in civil wars
and the Thirty Years War in Germany (1618–48) broke the ties of emperor to
pope. Protestants challenged Catholic monarchs, and even Charles I of
England, executed in 1649, was thought to have been too sympathetic to
Catholics, having married a Catholic and supported policies friendly to
Catholicism. Political upheavals were commonplace throughout Europe and
"religious wars," also commonplace, were creating such instability that it began
to dawn on wiser heads that some foundation for religious tolerance must put
a stop to these conflicts for the well-being of the social and political order. But
these religious wars, like the conflict between Protestant and Catholics in
Northern Ireland in the twentieth century, while involving of religion, were
about more than religion. They involved growing nationalism and political
conflict and economic frustrations along with religious resentments. In examining these conflicts, it is important to keep in mind how much the political and
the religious had been an inseparable reality for much of European history. The
division between the religious and secular had not yet been fashioned, so that
trying to separate out and lay blame for war at the feet of religion, Christianity
in particular, as if it were a cause of violence beyond other contributing causes

---

[85] David Edwards, *Christianity: The First Two Thousand Years* (Maryknoll, NY:
Orbis Books, 1977), 30.

[86] Robert Michael, "Luther, Luther Scholars, and the Jews," *Encounter*, Vol. 46, no
4 (Autumn 1985): 343–344.

of war and violence is to miss the mark. William Cavanaugh's claim that religious violence is a myth goes exactly to this point – not that religion is not and has not been involved in war and conflict, but that violence is so pervasive in human affairs that when it appears its causes are legion, and to identify religion, or the religion of Christianity, as an overarching cause of violence important and influential beyond other secular causes is without evidentiary support.[87] Joshua Wright has undertaken research that concluded that given the play of certain variables, such as belief in life after death, there is empirical justification for holding the view that the more religious people are, the less likely are they to justify, and thus participate in, violent acts.[88]

Realism and just war thinking – just war considered as an ethic based on a common moral agreement against solving conflicts with violence or force – and the pacifism found in nonviolent resistance stand as two options for dealing with injustice and evil and with the question of force – what kind of force is allowable for Christians to use. These two options, just war and pacifism, identify an enduring tension in Christian thought and action. The tension provokes challenges for both the just war advocate who must observe last resort criterion in light of the moral agreement, common to all persons of good will, that force ought not to be used to settle conflicts, and nonviolent resister pacifists who confront evil in the world and may encounter ruthless movements and proponents of violence and destruction who, if not stopped with a use of force beyond nonviolence, could go on to destroy innocent life and commit murder, the slaughter of innocents, genocide or even omnicide. The just war option as laid out here seems to be the reasoned and practical possibility for fashioning a response consistent with Christian values, for just war, taken as an ethic, holds that nonviolence must establish the foundations of conflict resolution. It furthermore says that if it appears the costs of continuing nonviolent resistance does not offer sufficient resistance to redress the injustice at issue, an exception to the just war foundation – that force ought not be used to settle conflicts – could be employed if the criteria of justice and restraint are satisfied. Just war as

William T. Cavanaugh, *The Myth of Religious Violence: Secular Ideology and the Roots of Modern Conflict* (Oxford: Oxford University Press, 2009).
Wright, "More Religion, Less Justification for Violence," 159–183.

a perspective adopted widely by Christians as consistent with Christian concerns for both justice and peace, embodies in one philosophical perspective the element of violence/nonviolence dialectic under consideration in this section. It affirms a principled nonviolent resistance to uses of force but refuses to absolutize that nonviolence in the face of injustice and evil. It also holds open a possible use of force, always rule governed and in accord with the demands of justice – the just war criteria – so that just war allows the possibility of justified uses of force and restrained uses of violence in the interest of restoring peace and addressing injustice. Thus does this element of a violence/nonviolence dialectic provide a valuable resource for Christian persons confronting injustice. Just war thinking built upon the moral agreement against using force is more than a restraint in the use of force, it is a form of practical pacifism that does not get caught in some of the difficult problems of theoretical absolute pacifism.

5 Identity

All of the elements under examination in this short study intersect with one another, which is to say that any particular illustration of an element has relevance to others. The "elements" selected here for discussion and examination hardly exhaust the many possibilities for access to the topic of Christianity and violence, and the two elements examined thus far are relevant to other elements that might be examined, including two identity-related issues that shall be examined in this section: 1. punishment and identity and 2. identity protection from perceived threats, especially from outside "others."

Punishment was a critical feature of both Augustine's and Aquinas' theory of just war, serving as a just cause for the use of force. Aquinas would quote Augustine: "A just war is wont to be described as one that avenges wrongs, when a nation or state has to be punished, for refusing to make amends for the wrongs inflicted by its subjects, or to restore what it has seized unjustly."[89] This just war punishment concern lives on wher

---

[89] Thomas Aquinas "Whether It Is Always Sinful to Wage War," in
Juergensmeyer and Kitts, eds., *Princeton Readings in Religion and Violence*
(Princeton: Princeton University Press, 2011), 43.

deliberations are conducted over humanitarian interventions or the prosecution of war criminals following a war where the aggressor, military leaders and even the aggressor state itself, now defeated, may face retribution and punishment from international tribunals. Christians have over the centuries used punishment violence to exercise social control and preserve Christian identity, not only with respect to individuals but, as this just war reference makes clear, also to nations. Attention will be given to the Christian use of punishment, especially the execution power, incarceration and the historical use of Inquisition against heresy and witchcraft.

Identity protection is also at issue in the second element examined in this section. Christian people, in preserving their identities both individually and communally, have engaged in the violence of slavery, racism and white supremacy; they have engaged in acts of terrorism; and they have operated in social and institutional structures dominated by patriarchal systems that perpetuate sexism and violence against women. At issue in this element are different ways Christian have resorted to violence with the ostensible purpose of advancing a vision of community believed to conform to Christian values. For those who resort to violence, the appeal to Christian values and violent action in response to a perceived threat to Christian identity are critically important. Acts of violence used to protect the community from perceived threats could be said to serve the end of attaining peace and social harmony – even just war thinking has classically aimed the violence of war toward this positive end. The problem, of course, is that resorting to violence contradicts that peaceful and harmonious end behaviorally, making such an end almost impossible to attain. Violence, after all, is likely to beget not peace and social harmony, but more violence.

Punishment, Social Control and Identity

Punishment and the Execution Power

Despite the fact that the founder of the religion of Christianity, Jesus of Nazareth, was found guilty of sedition by the Romans and executed as punishment for a crime against the state; and despite a Gospel story where an adulteress was about to be stoned for her sin until Jesus intervened and said "Let anyone among you who is without sin be the first throw a stone at her (John 8:3–11), thus saving the woman's life and repudiating the "eye for an eye" retribution ethic that the Hebrews had located in Leviticus 24.20 and which Leviticus had inherited from the Code of Hammurabi, Christians have long supported both the Church and the state imposing retributive punishments on those who violate law or Church teaching. That support of retribution has long included the execution power; and retribution, including that involved in execution, is an ethic still endorsed by many Christians today. The central justification for retribution as an ethic – retribution here meaning the infliction of harm and pain on an offender as a just penalty for the harm they have visited unjustly on others – is, for those seeking Biblical warrants, St. Paul's invocation of "the power of the Sword" discussed in Section 2.

Church and state had functionally intertwined when the Emperor Constantine converted to Christianity in the fourth century CE. Constantine's effort to bring peace to the Empire was advanced by his conversion to Christianity, and he comingled church and state by affirming as Emperor the Council of Nicaea's theological claim that Jesus was divine and of one substance with God the Father. In 380, Theodosius I, Emperor of the Eastern Roman Empire, went one step further. In the presence of Valentinian II, the Western Roman Emperor, Theodosius I signed the Edict of Thessalonica, which made Christianity the official state church of the Roman Empire, and that recognition allowed Christian institutions to exercise a political power, including a power to punish those identified as enemies of Christian faith and institutions. No clear church/state divide was in existence at this time – the division between secular and religious that put "legitimated" violence under governmental authority would not become established in Europe until the Enlightenment and the rise of secularism and nationalism. In the last two centuries of the Roman Empire, however, the state's power to inflict the violence of punishment on law-breaking offenders included those who violated Christian norms and directives as heretics or enemies of the Church. The state thus meted out punishment on behalf of the Church. Making Christianity the official state religion of the Roman Empire had, from its very beginning, involved persecuting nonbelievers and inflicting punishment on those committing the high treason of pagan rituals. The decree signed by Theodosius included these words:

> We authorize the followers of this law to assume the title of Catholic Christians; but as for the others, since, in our judgment they are foolish madmen, we decree that they shall be branded with the ignominious name of heretics, and shall not presume to give to their conventicles the name of churches.
>
> They will suffer in the first place the chastisement of the divine condemnation and in the second the punishment of our authority which in accordance with the will of Heaven we shall decide to inflict.[90]

Christians had been victims of Roman violence and oppression since the first century, especially during the reign of the Emperor Nero, who lit his garden walk with burning Christians as his torches. Executions in the Roman Empire had been in the main confined to slaves, common criminals, army deserters and prisoners of war, and those who killed a person beneath their status were exempt from any punishment. Executions were events that held significant entertainment value as public spectacle, with burning alive and crucifixion favored methods of dispatch.[91] Constantine's Edict of Milan in 315 brought religious tolerance to Christians and put an end to their persecution by the Roman authorities. With punishment and execution thoroughly ensconced in the violence of the Roman Empire, however, lethal retribution involving Christians was a natural consequence of the Christian Church acquiring status as a partner with the state. The

[90] Matthias von Hellfeld, "Christianity Becomes the Religion of the Roman Empire – February 27, 380," www.dw.com/en/christianity-becomes-the-religion-of-the-roman-empire-february-27-380/a-4602728.

Owlcation, "How and Why the Romans Executed People," June 8, 2016, https://owlcation.com/humanities/roman-executions-why-the-romans-executed-people.

subsequent recognition of Christianity as the official state religion of the Roman Empire reinforced this expression of political power.

That toleration did not extend with consistency to Jews. Because Jews were having success in bringing converts into their fold, Constantine and subsequent emperors made proselytizing by Jews a crime punishable by death.[92] The execution power of the Empire came to serve the Christian Church, which perceived a threat in the conversion activities of Jews. Christians to this day support use of the execution power not for theological offenses[93] but as an appropriate governmentally endorsed and legally sanctioned response to certain kinds of legal and moral offenses, such as aggravated murder. Worthy of note is that Roman Catholic Church leaders have since the early 1970s endorsed to varying degrees a "seamless garment of life" position, inspired by a pro-life position on the abortion issue, to affirm reverence for life; and capital punishment has over time been more fully accepted as a use of violence that, in the context of this broader ethic of reverence for life, has been shunned.

When it is grounded in the legitimate authority of a political state exercising through law a societal response to serious criminal offense, the execution power is expressed though the punishment option of capital punishment, which refers to a lethal punishment delivered through a criminal justice system. The Church's reliance on execution to punish heretics and witches was a way to assert the power of ecclesiastical authority as it upheld the integrity of the faith and its temporal power structure, the purity of belief and the well-being of the community. But Christians would not always confine themselves to a use of the execution power through the

---

[92] Marcel Simon, *Verus Israel: A Study of the Relations Between Christianity and Jews in the Roman Empire, AD 135–425*, trans. H. McKeating (Portland, OR: Liverpool University Press, 1986), 291–292.

[93] There have been contemporary Christians who have advocated death as a punishment for what they hold to be the sin of homosexuality. Americans United for Separation of Church and State, "Religious Right Activist Calls for Execution of Homosexuals, *Church and State*, February 2010. www.au.org /church-state/february-2010-church-state/people-events/religious-right-activist-calls-for-execution

sanctions of legitimate authority, meaning the institutions of the Church and the state acting in conjunction with the Church.

The execution power can be much broader than capital punishment. Executions can be taken up extra-legally by vigilantes, revolutionaries and groups that simply assert the power to execute persons deemed fit for execution due to some specified reason, like failing a test of loyalty or belonging to a group, or expressing or representing a viewpoint at odds with those claiming the execution power. We know from analyses of lynching in the American South in the nineteenth and twentieth centuries that public vigilante executions were expressions of community will rather than "the power of a distant and alien government. For this reason, modern executions are concentrated in those sections of the United States where the hangman used to administer popular justice without legal sanction."[94]

The legacy of extra-legal lynchings as community events that kept the community free of despoiling outsiders – Blacks – thus persisted. The lynchings of Blacks by white vigilantes in the United States represented the community gathering extra-legally to eliminate and punish individuals who were deemed offensive and a threat to the racial purity and the well-being of the majority white community. Christians were in those lynch parties, often as members of groups like the Ku Klux Klan, believing that they were defending community norms, which included Christian values. Lynchings in this sense were punishments for assumed violations that the community, by resorting to lynchings, believed did not require the protection of outside and alien law. As a matter of record, many lynchings in the American South over the post–Civil War decades took place in town squares right across from jails and courthouses with law enforcement officials offering a reassuring presence to the crowds.

Incarceration

Christians have also supported retributive punishments that fall short of execution, such as public humiliation, shunning, corporeal punishments and imprisonment. Christians can assert different viewpoints on punishment

Franklin E. Zimring, *The Contradictions of American Capital Punishment* (New York, Oxford: Oxford University Press, 2003), 89.

issues, with various and incommensurable viewpoints claiming a basis in Christian values and teachings. Christian clergy have long entered prisons to provide comfort and solace to prisoners, and prison chaplaincy is a career route, though not one often taken, for some clergy even today. Lay Christians find ways into prisons to provide help with problems like harassment and medical neglect – and thus incidental spiritual comfort as well – by joining organizations that seek dedicated volunteers, the Pennsylvania Prison Society being among the most notable and successful.

As some Christians support the death penalty while others oppose it, so too is opinion divided on a punishment as familiar as incarceration. Incarceration is not a problematic form of punishment for many Christians, but for other Christians, visiting the incarcerated becomes a Christian duty. Remembering St. Paul's imprisonment and heeding the teaching of Jesus to visit prisoners, some Christians, who have been to prison or who visit the incarcerated, know prisons to be sometimes cruel, violent and counterproductive environments where criminal intent and activity is often reinforced rather than eliminated. While efforts are always underway to improve incarceration, they are often stymied by local politics and budgets insufficient to invest in progressive corrections programming. In many American jails and prisons today, conditions are often distressing; corrections is not directed toward rehabilitation and inmates are not restored to meaningful citizenship. Accordingly, Christians can often be found at the forefront of prison reform movements.

Christian values have long been affirmed by those interested in improving systems of punishment. For instance, the first penitentiary in the United States was built in Philadelphia in 1829 by Quakers, whose roots are Christian, and it was designed to encourage penance on the part of offenders. Inmates were given work assignments and served their sentence in solitary confinement, a form of punishment now recognized to be particularly cruel, but reformers devised it originally as a replacement for corporeal punishment. Some Christians today support "decarceration efforts" that would do away with institutions like prisons and mental hospitals and reorganize society with more caring community-based ways to exercise social control and social well-being. Still, many Christians support the traditional punishments found in criminal justice systems. Christian support of traditional modes of punishment expresses concern for justice as well as respect for Biblical precedent, where punishments, including executions, were quite common: The Hebrew Bible imposes death for thirty-six capital offenses, though it is to be noted that many of those offenses were violations of religious purity rituals rather than moral offenses.

The Bible, which Christians honor as (at least) a handbook for action and direction, endorses retributive justice – that "eye for an eye" theory of justice repudiated by Jesus. Retribution is both harsh and brutish in its ostensible aim to inflict pain and even injury on the offender, who, by execution or imprisonment, is denied an opportunity to atone for wrongdoing and work constructively to make things right with a victim. Restorative justice movements that seek to replace retribution models with a community-based approach that brings offenders and victims together to repair the harm caused by an offense advance a more fitting position on punishment, one consistent with Christian values of care for the afflicted and concern for the welfare of those who afflict. Restorative justice attends to the losses experienced by victims of crime with the offender making active and positive contributions to "restore" victims to well-being, with offenders involving themselves in agreed-upon actions that improve the welfare of those they injured in their offense. Restorative justice is viewed as a constructive alternative to mass incarceration since it is most easily adopted where the offenses committed have been nonviolent. One need not be Christian to support restorative justice efforts but there seems to be widespread support for this contemporary reform among Christians concerned about the deep justice concerns related to mass incarceration.

Inquisition

f the Crusades can be viewed as the Church using violence to protect tself from external enemies, Inquisition was the Church resorting to violence to deal with internal threats to the well-being of the Christian community.

A Christian orthodoxy had to be established before Christian heresy ould arise, and by the fourth century CE, both were in place. t. Augustine, who had opposed the execution of heretics, is sometime alled the father of the Inquisition since he is the singular voice that equated dissention against the Church and its teachings with dissentions against the state, so that if anyone were condemned by the Church, the state could legitimately mete out the punishments determined by Church authority.[95] Augustine was of the view that God had led St. Paul to the light of Christianity by a use of force; therefore uses of force were legitimate uses of violence employed to preserve and protect the orthodox doctrines of the faith. On that understanding, and to achieve church unity, Augustine approved the use of force against heretics, and by "force" meant the various Roman methods of torture. When Priscillian, Bishop of Avila, was charged with witchcraft, tried and tortured, he along with his companions confessed to heresy and were then handed over to the state for execution. "The Church now had precedents for both witch hunting and for persecuting heretics, with a moral underpinning provided by St. Augustine."[96]

Heresy was a religious offense. Because the state was theocratic and heresy challenged that the authority of governmental rulers came from God, heresy was also considered treason. In the twelfth century, The Second Lateran Council (1139 CE) imposed imprisonment and confiscation of property for heretics, but in the following century, Emperor Frederick II issued this directive concerning heretics:

> Anyone who has been manifestly convicted of heresy by the bishop of his diocese shall at the bishop's request be seized immediately by the secular authorities of the place and delivered to the stake. If the judges think his life should be preserved, particularly to convict other heretics, they shall cut out the tongue of the one who has not hesitated to blaspheme against the Catholic faith and the name of God.[97]

[95] Universal Declaration of Rights: Christianity and Its Persecution of Heretics, http://heretication.info/_heretics.html.

[96] Ibid.

[97] Jean Comby, *How to Read Church History, Volume I: From the Beginning to the Fifteenth Century* (New York: Crossroads, 1992), 167.

Pope Gregory IX issued a papal bull, *Excommunicatus*, in 1231, that established the legal system internal to the church to try heresy cases, pronounce sentence and determine punishment – civil authorities would receive the cases and carry out the judgment of the ecclesiastical court.[98] Inquisition tribunals were in place in the next century, and the Dominican inquisitors were granted power by the pope to bring charges against suspected, even rumored, heretics. The purpose of the Inquisition was to suppress heresy, return accused heretics to good standing in the Catholic Church, then punish those who refused to recant their errors.[99] In the Spanish Inquisition, estimates are that a million people were killed, although numbers seem more reasonably to range from 30,000 to 300,000, with more recent claims being that these numbers were all exaggerated.[100] There is no doubt, however, that people accused of heresy in European inquisitions were killed.

The Spanish Inquisition, which lasted from 1478 to 1834, addressed not just theology but politics. It took into its embrace not only Christian heretics but Muslims, Jews and, in later developments, Protestants. Bogomils, Waldensians, Cathars and Lollards, were persecuted, as were those who threatened the stability of the government.[101] A name remembered today as synonymous with cruelty, Torquemada, came to assume the position of Grand Inquisitor, and while it is often put forth that he had no desire greater than to burn Jews and Protestants, scholars are of the view that "his whole endeavor was to make all Catholics be loyal Catholics; [and that] he never wanted to be Inquisitor General; [and] had nothing of megalomania about him."[102]

---

[98] McBrien, *Catholicism: A Study Guide*, 9.   [99] Ibid.

[00] Sophie Arie, *The Guardian*, June 15, 2004, "Historians Say Inquisition Wasn't that Bad," www.theguardian.com/world/2004/jun/16/artsandhumanities .internationaleducationnews#:~:text=Estimates%20of%20the%20number% 20killed,ranged%20from%2030%2C000%20to%20300%2C000. This article shares a research finding that indicates 1% of the 125,000 people tried in Spain were actually executed.

[01] David L. Edwards, *Christianity: The First Two Thousand Years*(Maryknoll, NY: Orbis Books, 1997), 43, 266–268.

[2] William Thomas Walsh, *Characters of the Inquisition* (Rockford, IL: Tan Books and Publishers, 1940, 1987), 162.

Torquemada actually enacted some reforms following the abuses of his predecessors, improving prisons and prison food – some prisoners under civil charges actually pretended to be heretics so they could be transferred to the well-lighted and ventilated houses in which prisoners of the Holy Office were held.[103] Yet there was cruelty. Torture was employed to encourage confessions from accused and convicted heretics, and Torquemada employed a torture akin to waterboarding: If the accused did not clarify contradictions or was suspected of withholding important information he "was stretched naked and tied with cords upon a very forbidding-looking *escalera*, or ladder. His nostrils were stopped, his jaws held apart by an iron prong, and a piece of linen placed loosely over his mouth. Into this cloth water was slowly poured, carrying it to the throat,"[104] giving the sensation of suffocation.

Protestants also punished heretics though ecclesiastical tribunals. In theocratic Geneva, John Calvin justified burning non-Trinitarian Michael Servetus to the stake by claiming the state's duty to establish "true religion." "The state exists," Calvin wrote, "so that idolatry, sacrilege of the name of God, blasphemies against his truth and other public offenses against religion may not emerge and may not be disseminated."[105] Heresy unchecked led to false doctrine, which destroyed souls and undermined the community of faith, which was the Church. The punishments of heretics expressed both a desire to preserve the integrity of an orthodox community while addressing the fear of divine wrath, since that could bring about the horrible consequences of famine, plague and war.

Thomas Aquinas had defended executions of the heretic "if the church gives up hope of his conversion and takes thought for the safety of others, by separating him from the church by sentence of excommunication, and, further, leaves him to the secular court, to be exterminated from the world by death."[106] Inquisitions and sentencing tribunals for punishment of heresy relied upon torture to extract confessions, sometimes resulting in mass

---

[103] Ibid., 163. [104] Ibid., 169

[105] John Calvin, *Defensio orthodoxae fidei*, in T. H. L. Parker, *John Calvin: A Biography* (Philadelphia: Westminster Press, 1975), 123.

[106] Aquinas, *Summa Theologica*, IIa, IIae, ii, art 3.

executions. Not only heresy but witchcraft also became an object of persecution. Protestants and Catholics seemed almost in competition in attacking the witchcraft problem. Luther said, "I would burn them all."[107] An eyewitness to the witchcraft persecutions noted that the Holy Office burned 30,000 witches who, "if left unpunished, would easily have brought the whole world to destruction."[108] Although the number of witches burned is not known – estimates range from hundreds of thousands to millions – the target of this persecution being women, this move made by male-dominated church authorities to exterminate women expressed a murderous act of repression that one historian has called "a vast holocaust."[109]

The violence as persons accused of subverting the orthodoxy of a church or church community were tortured, condemned and executed is a lasting legacy of the Christian church. The Church inflicted punishments in order to preserve its identity and integrity, yet by these very acts they inflicted the violence that would ensure further subversion.

The Preservation of Identity: Slavery/Race/Terror

White Supremacy

Slavery, whether based on sex, race, status following a war or indebtedness is a violent social, political and economic institution that robs people of their labor and the very dignity of their humanity. It renders human beings property subject to disposal by others. It so bends them to the will of slaveholders and owners that slaves are often regarded as subhuman. They become targets of physical violence and abuse, which was certainly the case with slavery in America. Christians have held a variety of positions on slavery, and the context here is the American experience, where slavery and the slave trade was legalized from before the founding of the constitutional government.

Those who defended slavery turned to passages in the New Testament. For example, St. Paul writes in Ephesians 6.5–8, "Slaves, obey your earthly masters with fear and trembling, in singleness of heart as you obey

---

[7] McBrien, 122. [108] Ibid., 127. [109] Ibid., 126.

Christ,"[110] and in the letter to Philemon in the New Testament, urges Philemon to return a fugitive slave Onesimus and to regard the slave as a brother in Christ and not as a slave. Paul does not condemn the institution of slavery, and the manumission of slaves was not uncommon in St. Paul's day since slavery was so established as a form of servitude that were a slave's debt to be paid, the slave could be freed without enormous controversy. A person's status as slave was not as important to St. Paul as the person's Christian identity, and he invoked language to indicate the appropriateness of thinking of one's identity as being a "slave" to Christ. In 1 Corinthians 7.21 St. Paul writes:

> Were you a slave when called? Do not be concerned about it.
> Even if you can gain your freedom, make use of your present
> condition now more than ever. For whoever was called in the
> Lord as a slave is a freed person belonging to the Lord, just as
> whoever was free when called is a slave of Christ. (NRSV)

As one who avowed Christianity as an eschatological faith, St. Paul believed history itself was coming to an end and that Christ was coming again: Paul expected that return soon. This may account for Paul's attitudes toward slavery and perhaps even marriage (he is not encouraging of it) because if all is going to end soon (as in day after tomorrow), the transitory circumstances of human life prior to Christ's return ought not be distractions from the momentous change that will occur when Christ does return. How that will happen Paul discusses in his earliest letter, 1 Thessalonians. Many passages in St. Paul emphasize freedom in Christ – the Letter to the Galatians is a paean to freedom and to eliminating distinctions between persons: In Christ, he writes, "There is no longer Jew nor Greek, there is no longer slave nor free, there is no longer male or female" (Galatians 3.28 NRSV). Liberation will attend Christ's return, and one's situation, oppressive though it may be now, will be transformed into freedom for those baptized into the faith where all persons are equal before God.

---

[110] Similar sentiments are found in Col. 3.22–24; 1 Timothy 6.1–2; and Titus 2.9–10.

The problem with these different Biblical messages concerning interpretations of slavery, however, is that they would come to dominate much of the political debate over slavery and the slavery economy in antebellum America. If abolitionists emphasized that human beings were created in God's image and slavery reduced human beings to property, proslavery advocates quoted Philemon and other passages where it seems that Paul at least condoned slavery, certainly coming up short of condemning the institution. So defenders of slavery – this is the horrendously cruel chattel slavery of the American south[111] – claimed to have the Bible on their side in support of their economic and social system – their way of life; and many a Sunday morning in white Southern Protestant churches, preachers could be expected to defend and even extol slavery to their congregations, thus creating a moral impasse with abolitionists and other slavery opponents who turned to Scripture and Christian values to condemn the institution.

American slavery was based in race. The Christianity that slavery advocates affirmed was also based in race. White Christians distinguished Black slaves from the agent of their salvation, Jesus Christ, racializing Jesus as white, which in many ways continues to this day in American Christianity. Robert P. Jones offers this account:

> There are no descriptions of Jesus' physical characteristics in the gospels, and what we do know – that he was Jewish and from the Middle East – easily makes nonsense of any claims that Jesus shared with white American Christians a European heritage. But from the white European point of view, shot through with colonialist assumptions about racial hierarchies and white supremacy, there was no other possible conclusion.

[11] Slavery did exist in the Northern states prior to its elimination in 1804, and then was eliminated nationwide with the adoption of the Thirteenth Amendment in 1865. Slaves were noted in the 1840 census in the North. Northern businessmen made investments and gained financially from the slave trade and plantation agriculture, so the whole nation was involved in maintaining and perpetuating slavery, though the direct cruelties visited on human persons as slaves occurred overwhelmingly in the American South.

The story of human salvation had to find expression in
a divinely ordained, hierarchical universe. As the exemplar
of what it meant to be perfectly human, Jesus by definition
had to be white. Whites simply couldn't conceive of owing
their salvation to a representative of what they considered an
inferior race. And a nonwhite Jesus would render impossible
the intimate relationalism necessary for the evangelical para-
digm to function: no proper white Christian would let
a brown man come into their hearts or submit themselves to
be a disciple of a swarthy Semite.[112]

Slavery was an egregious crime the legacy of which persists today in all
kinds of social inequities, dislocations and stiflings of opportunity for Blacks.
Historically, Christian people, in defending slavery, and then in supporting
social, political and economic doctrines of "separate but equal" along with
broadly racialized attitudes of anti-Black sentiment have contributed to the
violence of white supremacy in what has developed in the United States
empirically as a racially pluralistic society. White Christians are often found
opposing affirmative action; and on instruments that measure racial resentment whites have shown that those who reside in areas that had the highest
levels of slavery in 1860 have significantly different attitudes from whites who
reside in areas that had lower level of slavery historically, leading researchers
to conclude "present-day regional differences, then, are the direct down-
stream consequences of the slaveholding history of these areas."[113] Efforts to
put slavery "behind us" and move everyone into a nonracialized colorblind
society – a dubious objective yet one advanced by many whites – seems in the
current state of affairs to be doomed to failure. High level political figures
have in recent times provoked a sense of legitimacy for racial resentment as
the racial divide in America is reset and violence against Blacks is unleashed.
The research previously quoted was on white Americans, but those white
Americans are, many of them, Christians, and Christian people and their

[112] Robert P. Jones, *White Too Long: The Legacy of White Supremacy in American Christianity* (New York: Simon and Schuster, 2020): 101.

[113] Ibid., 156.

Christian institutions have acted over the centuries to perpetuate these attitudes of prejudice and white supremacy.

The leadership of the civil rights movement in America attacked white supremacy and the "separate but equal" legal doctrines that failed to deliver social and political equality for Blacks. That leadership came from the Christian churches and there is no doubt that American Christians, including white Christians, have supported efforts to dismantle white supremacy. There will continue to be support from Christian churches and Christian men and women in this effort. The problem is that victory over something as invidious as white supremacy can be declared too soon, and hugely symbolic moves such as the election of the first Black American president can obscure the depth of the racial divide and lead to the mistaken view that a colorblind society has been achieved. Whether such an end should even be an aim of efforts at achieving racial justice is, as just mentioned, a highly dubious claim[114] – the legacy of slavery is a constant in American life, and some Christians have perpetuated white supremacy while others have worked toward its dismantling. Racial policies that first enslaved and then subjected Blacks to second-class citizenship status have found support from Christians who have felt their Christian communities – their Christian identities – threatened by racial diversity. They have, over the centuries, created in those communities – those churches – places for asserting white supremacist values as Christian values. They have resorted to violence to protect their identity as Christians, by which is meant, white Christians.

Christian Terrorists

Another place to look for Christians acting violently in defense of their identities as Christian is in an activities category we could call "Christian terrorism." Although an unusual and rarely used designation, there have been Christians who, in defense of what they hold to be overwhelmingly

---

[114] The work of Michelle Alexander is not only to address the problem of race and mass incarceration but to explode the myth that a colorblind society is appropriate as a goal in seeking to establish racial equality. See Michelle Alexander, *The New Jim Crow: Mass Incarceration in the Age of Colorblindness* (New York: The New Press, 2010).

important Christian values, have resorted to violence to advance an extremist agenda, and two examples are worthy of note.

The first is the abortion clinic bomber and the abortion doctor killer.

Abortion has been a major – for some Christians, "the" major – social and political issue of the past fifty years. Although not particularly associated with conservatism or liberalism politically, abortion climbed up the social concerns agenda first because of the papal document *Humanae Vitae* (1968) and then as a major issue in the 1980 presidential campaign. Abortion views have proved to be an unprecedented influence over public attitudes and social policy. The Roman Catholic Church has opposed all abortions, and anti-abortion positions that were originally modified and restrictive "choice" positions in that they made exceptions for rape, incest and abortion to save a woman's life have been abandoned as attitudes have become more extreme, with these "exceptions" playing less of a role in anti-abortion thinking and even in legal initiatives in the United States. Today, despite Christian majority organizations such as the Religious Coalition for Reproductive Choice and denominational statements from progressive Protestant churches supporting reproductive freedom of choice, many evangelical Protestant Christians have joined with Catholics in a fierce opposition to abortion. And the issue has attracted extremists.

A Lutheran Pastor, Michael Bray, is a leading spokesperson for a Christian extremism concerning anti-abortion activities. Editor of *Capitol Area Christian News*, Bray has advocated destruction of abortion service facilities and was convicted and sentenced to prison for four years for destroying seven abortion clinics in Delaware, Maryland and Virginia. He defended Paul Hill's murder of an abortion provider and escort in Pensacola, Florida – Hill was sentenced to death and executed for the crime – and another of Bray's colleagues was responsible for the killing of Dr. George Tiller in Wichita, Kansas.

Bray's defense of his murderous extremism is explicitly grounded in Christian values and interpretation. He has written,

> What is the Christian's role, What do the Scriptures say? . . .
> Surely our lamb-carrying Jesus couldn't have been approving them! Could he?

> Yes. He could. That is the short answer. This Jesus – the same yesterday, today, and forever (Heb. 13:8) – is the "man of War" of the Scriptures. He is the God of Israel who wrought calamity upon Israel as well as her enemies. He is not squeamish about destruction and war. The One who uses force and consecrates others to do the same does not have a problem with it.[115]

And he goes on to say, "This is the God who slays his apostate people with pestilence (1 Chronicles 21.2–16) . . . This is our Lord Jesus. He has no problem with the use of force and bloodshed. He has a big problem with the shedding of innocent blood, however" (Prov. 6.16, 17).[116]

The viewpoints expressed here, the explicit deference to a Christian justification for murderous activities, allow use of the tag "Christian terrorist" to be applied to Bray, Paul Hill and others who advocate this kind of anti-abortion violence. It should be noted that Bray defends his actions not only by Scriptural warrants of justification, but by appeal to the idea that his cause is righteous and his war on abortion providers is a just war, or, in his words, a "righteous rebellion."[117] Bray is the probable author of an underground manual of the Army of God, "which specifies how to undertake terrorist attacks," and he has defended his acts of terror in the book, *A Time to Kill.*[118]

Extremist groups like the Army of God, Operation Rescue and Christian Identity represent extremist groups advocating violence in defense of a Christian identity. The Christian Identity movement is grounded in a view combining racial supremacy with biblical injunctions. The theology of the Christian Identity movement is racist and anti-Semitic, and its core belief is that white people, not Jews, are the true Israelites favored by God in the Bible. Fundamentalists who hold that the return of Jesus to Israel is

---

[15] Michael Bray, "A Time for Revolution? A Time to Kill," in Juergensmeyer and Kitts, eds., *Princeton Readings in Religion and Violence* (Princeton, Oxford: Princeton University Press, 2011), 59.

[16] Ibid., 60.

[17] Mark Juergensmeyer, *Terror of the Mind of God: The Global Rise of Religious Violence*, 3rd ed. (Berkeley: University of California Press, 2003), 30.

[18] Ibid.

necessary for the Second Coming of Christ have kept their distance from the Christian Identity movement, but the movement has been influential and has affected American extremist movements like Posse Comitatus, the Order, the Aryan Nations, The Worldwide Church of God, the Freeman Compound and the World Church of the Creator.[119] Although a professed atheist, Oklahoma City bomber Timothy McVeigh was very much influenced by Christian Identity publications and may have had some contact with leaders in that organization.[120] The Southern Poverty Law Center has noted in recent years a decline in the number of Christian terror or hate groups and a list of them can be found on their web site.[121]

Christian extremists who resort to violence to oppose governmental actions believed to be contrary to the will of God or to oppose practices they find ungodly (i.e., abortion) will resort to killing and mayhem, justifying it – as Bray did – as action consistent with the divine will and authorized by God. In the extremist effort, persons like Bray or Paul Hill, or supporters of the Christian Identity movement, will act to oppose what they believe is evil and in so doing preserve their identity as Christians being faithful to core Christian values where God's wrath can, though their agency, be delivered on those who defy God's will. It is sometimes difficult to see the effort that is being made to preserve and defend a vision of a Christian world or to uphold a stance whereby Christian values are recognizable as consistent with more traditional mainstream Christian values related to peace, love and forgiveness.

6 Concluding Remarks

The elements discussed in this final section are selective and somewhat arbitrary in their presentation. Although we focused here on white

---

[119] Ibid., 31. [120] Ibid.

[121] Southern Poverty Law Center, "Christian Identity," www.splcenter.org/fight ing-hate/extremist-files/ideology/christian-identity. For background on the Christian Identity Movement, see Julius H. Bailey, "Fearing Hate: Reexamining the Media Coverage of the Christian Identity Movement," *Journal for the Study of Radicalism*, vol. 4, no. 1 (2010): 55–73. JSTOR, www.jstor.org/stable/ 41887644. Accessed 6 Nov. 2020.

supremacy, we could have as well focused on missionary movements, other Christian involvement in hate-terror groups like the Ku Klux Klan, and, of particular relevance today, gender affirmation resentments, anti–gay/lesbian/transgender discrimination and exclusion, and the patriarchal values that have inflicted violence upon women in the fold of Christian community. Although witchcraft executions were mentioned, much could be said about the institutional Church preserving social structures that prevent women from participating fully in the life of the Christian community – one thinks of the problem of women's ordination in Roman Catholicism and the teachings that subordinate women to men with the approval of church leaders and that inevitably perpetuate the institutional hierarchy.

Some of these issues of women's oppression are being addressed and have been undergoing scrutiny for some time, but the Church, being a slow mover and reluctant to change and very wary of taking on issues having to do with sexual ethics and identity, has a long way to go in all three of the Christianities: Protestantism, Roman Catholicism and Orthodoxy. Yet the subordination of women is a place ripe for investigation of violence in Christianity. Attention could also have identified the elements of violence in ritual, missionary movements, the whole phenomenon of martyrdom and many others. The effort here has been to identify the lengths to which Christians can go to preserve identity and to articulate elements of the Christianity and violence dialectic to show that the relationship between the two concepts is complex, never one-sided, and always open to investigation and moral critique.

Mark Juergensmeyer, who has contributed so much to the contemporary understanding of religion and violence, offers these words, which sum up in many ways the broader theme of this volume: "despite its central tenets of love and peace, Christianity – like most traditions – has always had a violent side."[122] As it is shortsighted to focus on the violence to the exclusion of Christianity's more positive contributions to culture and world spirituality, so too is it wrong to ignore the violence Christian people have committed and justified. It is necessary for Christians to confront that legacy of violence if they are going to bring to the world those core transformative values so critical to their faith tradition: love, forgiveness and peace.

---

[2] Juergensmeyer, *Terror in the Mind of God*, 19.

Bibliography

Alexander, Michelle. *The New Jim Crow: Mass Incarceration in the Age of Colorblindness*. New York: The New Press, 2010.

Americans United for Separation of Church and State. "Religious Right Activist Calls for Execution of Homosexuals." *Church and State*, February 2010. www.au.org/church-state/february-2010-church-state/people-events/religious-right-activist-calls-for-execution.

Anonymous, *Eyewitness to History.com*, "Nero Persecutes Christians 64 A. D." www.eyewitnesstohistory.com/christians.htm.

Aquinas, Saint Thomas, "On War," *Summa Theologica, II, II Q. 40*. Trans. Fathers of the English Dominican Province. Chicago: Encyclopedia Britannica, 1952.

Aquinas, Saint Thomas, Whether It Is Permissible to Kill a Man in Self-Defense?" *Summa Theologica, II-II, Q. 64 article 7*. Reprinted in *The Ethics of War: Classic and Contemporary Readings*, Gregory Reichberg, Henrik Syse and Endre Begby, eds. Malden, MA: Blackwell, 2006, 169–91.

Aquinas, Thomas. "Whether It Is Always Sinful to Wage War." In Mark Jurgensmeyer and Margo Kitts, eds. *Princeton Readings in Religion and Violence*. Princeton: Princeton University Press, 2011.

Arie, Sophie. "Historians Say Inquisition Wasn't that Bad." *The Guardian*, June 15, 2004. www.theguardian.com/world/2004/jun/16/artsandhumanities.internationaleducationnews#:~:text=Estimates%20of%20the%20number%20killed,ranged%20from%2030%2C000%20to%20300%2C000.

Armstrong, Karen. *Holy War: The Crusades and Their Impact on Today's World*. New York: Anchor Books, 1988, 2001.

Armstrong, Karen. *Battle for God*. New York: Alfred A Knopf, 2000.

Augustine, St. *Contra Fauastum Manichaeum*. In John Langan, "The Elements of St. Augustine's Just War Theory." *The Journal of Religious Ethics*, Vol. 12, no. 1 (Spring 1984).

Bailey, Julius H. "Fearing Hate: Reexamining the Media Coverage of the Christian Identity Movement." *Journal for the Study of Radicalism*, Vol. 4, no. 1 (2010): 55–73. JSTOR, www.jstor.org/stable/41887644. Accessed 6 Nov. 2020.

Bardon, Adrian. " Coronavirus Responses Highlight How Humans Have Evolved to Dismiss Facts that Don't Fit Their Worldview." *Scientific American, The Conversation US* (June 26, 2020). www.scientificamerican .com/article/coronavirus-responses-highlight-how-humans-have-evolved-to-dismiss-facts-that-dont-fit-their-worldview/.

Bray, Michael. "A Time for Revolution? A Time to Kill." In Mark Juergensmeyer and Margo Kitts, eds. *Princeton Readings in Religion and Violence*. Princeton, Oxford: Princeton University Press, 2011.

Calvin, John. *Defensio orthodoxae fidei*. In T. H. L. Parker, ed. *John Calvin: A Biography*. Philadelphia: Westminster Press, 1975.

Carlson, John D. "Religion and Violence: Coming to Terms with Terms." In Andrew R. Murphy, ed. *Blackwell Companion to Religion and Violence*. West Sussex, UK: Wiley Blackwell, 2011, 14–18.

Carroll, James. *Constantine's Sword: The Church and the Jews, A History*. New York: Mariner Books, Houghton Mifflin, 2001.

Cavanaugh, William T. *The Myth of Religious Violence: Secular Ideology and the Roots of Modern Conflict*. Oxford: Oxford University Press, 2009.

Coady, C. A. J. "Violence and Religion." *Revue Internationale de Philosophie*, Vol. 67, no. 265(3) (2013): 237–257.

Comby, Jean. *How to Read Church History, Volume I: From the Beginning to the Fifteenth Century*. New York: Crossroads, 1992.

Edwards, David. *Christianity: The First Two Thousand Years*. Maryknoll, NY: Orbis Books, 1977.

Edwards, David L. *Christianity: The First Two Thousand Years*. Maryknoll, NY: Orbis Books, 1997.

Gottfried, Robert S. *The Black Death: Natural and Human Disaster in Medieval Europe*. New York: The Free Press, 1983.

Grotius, Hugo. "The Theory of Just War Systematized (On the Law of War and Peace)." Reprinted in *The Ethics of War: Classic and Contemporary Readings*, Gregory Reichberg, Henrick Syse and Endre Begby, eds. Malden, MA: Blackwell, 2006, 385–437. www.splcen ter.org/fighting-hate/extremist-files/ideology/christian-identity

Isaac, Matthew. "Sacred Violence or Strategic Faith? Disentangling the Relationship between Religion and Violence in Armed Conflict." *Journal of Peace Research*, Vol. 53, no. 2 (February 2016): 211–225. https://doi .org/10.1177/0022343315626771.

Jenkins, Philip. "A Most Violent Year: The World into which Jesus was Born." www.abc.net.au/religion/a-most-violent-year-the-world-into-which-jesus-was-born/10097496.

Jenkins. Philip. *Jesus Wars: How Four Patriarchs, Three Queens, and Two Emperors Decided What Christians Would Believe for the Next 1,500 Years*. New York: HarperOne, 2011.

Jones, Robert P. *White Too Long: The Legacy of White Supremacy in American Christianity*. New York: Simon and Schuster, 2020.

Juergensmeyer, Mark. *Terror of the Mind of God: The Global Rise of Religious Violence*, 3rd ed. Berkeley: University of California Press 2003.

Kelly, John. *The Great Mortality: An Intimate History of the Black Death* London, New York: Harper Perennial, 2005, 2006, 2013.

King, Martin Luther, Jr. "Playboy Interview." In *Testament of Hope: The Essential Writings and Speeches*. New York: Harper and Row, 2003.

Krech, Volkhard. "Sacrifice and Holy War: A Study of Religion and Violence." In Wilhelm Heitmeyer and John Hagan, eds. *International Handbook of Violence Research*. Dordrecht: Kluwer Academic Publishers, 1005–1021.

Lincoln, Bruce. *Holy Terrors: Thinking about Religion after September 11*. Chicago: University of Chicago Press, 2002.

McBrien, Richard. *Catholicism: A Study Guide*. Minneapolis: Winston Press, 1981.

Menonite Church USA, "Article 22. Peace, Justice, and Nonresistance." At www.mennoniteusa.org/who-are-mennonites/what-we-believe/confession-of-faith/peace-justice-and-nonresistance/.

Michael, Robert. "Luther, Luther Scholars, and the Jews." *Encounter*, Vol. 46 no.4 (Autumn 1985), 343–344.

Moser, Caroline O. N., and Dennis Rodgers. "Working Paper 245: Change, Violence and Insecurity in Non-Conflict Situations." London: Overseas Development Institute, March 2005. www.odi.org/sites/odi.org.uk/files/odi-assets/publications-opinion-files/1824.pdf.

Nelson, Lynn. "The Great Famine (1315–1317)/and the Black Death (1346–1351)." *Lectures in Medieval History, 2001*. www.vlib.us/medieval/lectures/black_death.html.

Niebuhr, Reinhold. "Why the Christian Church Is Not Pacifist." In Mark Juergensmeyer and Margo Kitts, eds. and introduction. *Princeton Readings in Religion and Violence*, Princeton: Princeton University Press, 2011, 46.

ohl, Johannes. *The Black Death: A Chronicle of the Plague*. Trans. C. H. Clarke. New York: J. & J. Harper, 1924, 2006.

oyes, George Rapall. *Tolstoy*. New York: Dover, 1968.

wlcation, "How and Why the Romans Executed People." June 8, 2016. https://owlcation.com/humanities/roman-executions-why-the-romans-executed-people.

Parry, Wynne. "Molecular Clues Hint at What Really Caused the Black Death." *Live Science* (September 7, 2011). www.livescience.com/15937-black-death-plague-debate.html.

Ruia, Teofilo F. "Medieval Europe: Crisis and Renewal," *An Age of Crisis: Hunger.* The Teaching Company. ISBN 1-56585-710-0, cited in https://en.wikipedia.org/wiki/Great_Famine_of_1315%E2%80%931317.

Sandmel, Samuel. *Anti-Semitism in the New Testament.* Philadelphia: Fortress, 1978.

Shields, Christopher, and Daniel Schwartz, "Francisco Suárez." In Edward N. Zalta, ed. *The Stanford Encyclopedia of Philosophy* (Winter 2019 Edition). https://plato.stanford.edu/archives/win2019/entries/suarez/.

Simon, Marcel. *Verus Israel: A Study of the Relations Between Christianity and Jews in the Roman Empire, AD 135-425.* Trans. H. McKeating. Portland, OR: Liverpool University Press, 1986.

Southern Poverty Law Center. "Christian Identity." www.splcenter.org/fighting-hate/extremist-files/ideology/christian-identity.

Steffen, Lloyd. *Executing Justice: The Moral Meaning of the Death Penalty.* Eugene, OR: Wipf & Stock, 2006.

Steffen, Lloyd. *Holy War, Just War: Exploring the Moral Meaning of Religious Violence*, Lanham, MD: Rowman and Littlefield, 2007.

Steffen, Lloyd. "Gandhi's Nonviolent Resistance: A Justified Use of Force?" *Journal of Philosophy and the Contemporary World*, Vol. 15, no. 1 (June 2008): 68-80.

Tolstoy, Leo. "The Law of Love and the Law of Violence." In *A Confession and Other Religious Writings.* Trans Jane Kentish. Harmondsworth, UK Penguin Books, 1987.

Universal Declaration of Rights: Christianity and Its Persecution of Heretics http://heretication.info/_heretics.html.

von Hellfeld, Matthias. "Christianity Becomes the Religion of the Roman Empire – February 27, 380." www.dw.com/en/christianity-becomes-the-religion-of-the-roman-empire-february-27-380/a-4602728.

Walsh, William Thomas. *Characters of the Inquisition*. Rockford, IL: Tan Books and Publishers, 1940, 1987.

Walton, Hanes, Jr. "King's Philosophy of Nonviolence." In Thomas Siebold, ed. *Martin Luther King Jr*. San Diego: Greenhaven Press, 2000.

Wernock, Adam. "How Science Denial on the Political Right Hampers the US Response to Covid-19." *The World* (April 22, 2020). www.pri.org/stories/2020-04-22/how-science-denial-political-right-hampers-us-response-covid-19.

Wright, Joshua D. "More Religion, Less Justification for Violence: A Cross-National Analysis." *Archive for the Psychology of Religion*, Vol. 38, no. 2 (2016): 159–183.

Yoder, John Howard. *The Politics of Jesus*. Grand Rapids, MI: Eerdmans, 1972.

ZENIT Daily Dispatch, "St. Francis and Christian-Muslim Relations, Interview with Lawrence Cunningham." 29 March 2006. www.ewtn.com/catholicism/library/st-francis-and-christianmuslim-relations-1631.

Ziegler, Philip. *The Black Death*. New York: Harper Perennial, 2009.

Zimring, Franklin E. *The Contradictions of American Capital Punishment*. New York, Oxford: Oxford University Press, 2003.

Cambridge Elements ≡

Religion and Violence

James R. Lewis
Wuhan University

James R. Lewis is Professor at Wuhan Univesity, and the
author and editor of a number of volumes, including *The
Cambridge Companion to Religion and Terrorism*.

Margo Kitts
Hawai'i Pacific University

Margo Kitts edits the *Journal of Religion and Violence* and is
Professor and Coordinator of Religious Studies and East-West
Classical Studies at Hawai'i Pacific University in Honolulu.

ABOUT THE SERIES

Violence motivated by religious beliefs has become all too common
in the years since the 9/11 attacks. Not surprisingly, interest in the
topic of religion and violence has grown substantially since then.
This Elements series on Religion and Violence addresses this new,
frontier topic in a series of fifty individual Elements. Collectively, the
volumes will examine a range of topics, including violence in major
world religious traditions, theories of religion and violence, holy
war, witch hunting, and human sacrifice, among others.

Cambridge Elements ≡

Religion and Violence

Printed in the United States
by Baker & Taylor Publisher Services